The Devlin Family in Philadelphia

Descended from

Peter Devlin

Born c 1810 in Ireland

(the female perspective)

The Devlin Family in Philadelphia

Descended from

Peter Devlin

Born c 1810 in Ireland

(the female perspective)

Kathryn Chambers Torpey
Alexandria, Virginia

Kathryn Chambers Torpey is a professional genealogist and researcher. She is certified by the Board for Certification of Genealogists[SM].

Other Books by Kathryn Chambers Torpey:

John Kennedy of County Donegal, Ulster, Ireland, and His Descendants - A Compiled Genealogy (Including Risk, McCoy, and Pendleton), 2006

William Kennedy of Chester County, Pennsylvania, and His Descendants - A Compiled Genealogy (Including Davis, Smith, Wallace, Russell, and McClure), 2014

Colonial and Revolutionary Kennedy Families from Southeastern Pennsylvania, 2015

The Edwards/Scott Family History - Edinburgh to Philadelphia, 2016

The Chambers Family in Philadelphia Descended from George Chambers Born c 1815 in Ireland, 2016

The Reitze Family in Philadelphia Descended from Christopher Reitze Born 1824 in Hesse-Cassel, Germany, 2017

Imprint: CreateSpace Independent Publishing Platform

ISBN-13: 978-1717010599
ISBN-10: 1717010598

Torpey Books
5035 Domain Place
Alexandria, VA
22311-5066

In memory of my father,
William Scott Chambers

Contents

Appendices

FOREWORD

This family history documents what is known about the Devlin family in Philadelphia descended from Peter Devlin who was born circa 1810 in Ireland. The narrative is presented from the perspective of Susan (Kennedy) Devlin, the wife of Peter Devlin.

The first part of the narrative concerns Susan (Kennedy) Devlin's great-grandparents, her grandparents, and her parents most of whom were of Scots-Irish Presbyterian ancestry. The second part of the narrative concerns Susan (Kennedy) Devlin's husband, Peter Devlin, and their six children. It includes information about the origins of Peter Devlin in Ireland, his decision to leave home, his arrival in America, and the life of the Devlin family after his marriage to Susan Kennedy.

The original family tree was compiled by my father, William Scott Chambers, in the 1950s from oral information he obtained from his grandmother, Josephine (Reitze) Chambers, the granddaughter of Peter and Susan (Kennedy) Devlin.

The research contained in this family history was conducted between 1995 and 2018 in Washington, D.C., at the National Archives, the Library of Congress, and the Daughters of the American Revolution Library. Substantial research was also conducted at the McLean Family History Center and the National Genealogical Society Library both then located in Northern Virginia.

Other repositories that were visited included the Free Library of Philadelphia, the Philadelphia City Archives, the Genealogical Society of Pennsylvania, and the Historical Society of Pennsylvania all located in Philadelphia; the Friends Historical Library of Swarthmore College in Swarthmore, Pennsylvania; the Chester County Historical Society in West Chester, Pennsylvania; the Camden County Historical Society in Camden, New Jersey; and the Gloucester County Historical Society in Woodbury, New Jersey.

Site visits were made to the Upper and Lower Burial Grounds of the Forks of the Brandywine Presbyterian Church in Glenmoore, Pennsylvania and to the former Kennedy Plantation in West Caln Township, Chester County, Pennsylvania. Additional site visits were made to Old Cathedral Cemetery and New Cathedral Cemetery both located in Philadelphia; Lawnview Cemetery located in Rockledge as well as to the Pennsylvania Memorial located at the National Military Park in Gettysburg, Pennsylvania.

In addition, correspondence was carried out with several institutions and facilities including the Philadelphia Archdiocesan Historical Research Center and the Catholic Cemeteries Office in Philadelphia; the Chester County Archives in West Chester, Pennsylvania; and the York County Archives in York, Pennsylvania.

Extensive interviews were conducted with the late William Scott Chambers, the late Josephine Thompson Marshall, and John Joseph Page, three of the great-great-grandchildren of

Peter and Susan (Kennedy) Devlin, and with David Harrington Marshall, Jr., one of their great-great-great-grandsons.

Contact was established and information was exchanged with Russell Vance Kennedy, a great-great-great-great-great-grandson of William and Susanna (Doak) Kennedy who descends collaterally from their son, Samuel Kennedy, and his son, William Doak Kennedy. Mr. Kennedy is a family historian who researched the Kennedy family for more than ten years. He is in possession of the genealogical research material generated by his great-grandfather, Samuel Ridgway Kennedy, and his great-aunt, Edna Letitia Kennedy Haydock, including the *Kennedy Family Bible* published circa 1846. Mr. Kennedy provided a copy of the Revolutionary War Service Certification for William Kennedy as well as a sworn statement concerning the origin of the Kennedy family information that appears in Joseph Smith Harris' book entitled *Record of the Smith Family Descended from John Smith Born 1655 in County Monaghan, Ireland.* Both documents appear in the appendix. Mr. Kennedy also applied to the Veterans Administration for a flat granite War of 1812 marker that was placed on the grave of his great-great-great-grandfather, William Doak Kennedy, at Lawnview Cemetery on November 3, 1986.

A debt of gratitude is due to the late Joseph Smith Harris (1836-1910) author of *Record of the Smith Family Descended from John Smith Born 1655 in County Monaghan, Ireland,* and to the late Edna Letitia Kennedy Haydock (1882-1985) author of *The Kennedy Family,* both of whom undertook the difficult task of bringing together what could be gathered during their lifetime so that it could be printed and preserved before it could be forgotten.

Finally, it should be noted that, even though the family legend concerning the Quaker heritage of Susan Kennedy has not been proven, this family legend was handed down for generations by descendants of Lucy (Devlin) Reitze's children who were not in contact with each other for more than fifty years. For that reason, the appendix to this family history presents the Quaker legend as well as the factual foundation for the legend should additional avenues of exploration become available at a later date.

Kathryn Chambers Torpey
April 10, 2018

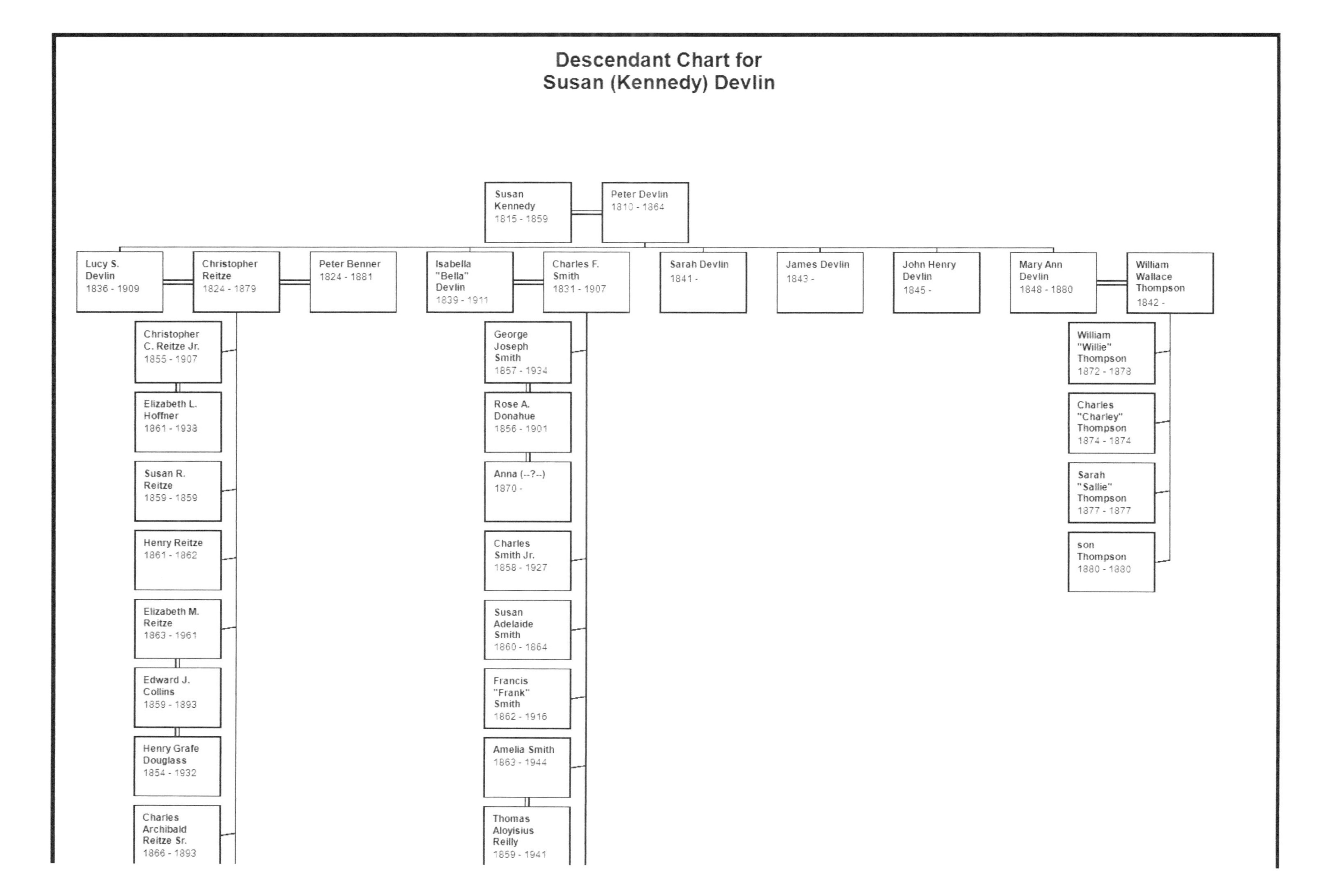

Descendant Chart for
Susan (Kennedy) Devlin

Susan Kennedy 1815 - 1859
Peter Devlin 1810 - 1864

Lucy S. Devlin 1836 - 1909
Christopher Reitze 1824 - 1879
Peter Benner 1824 - 1881
Isabella "Bella" Devlin 1839 - 1911
Charles F. Smith 1831 - 1907
Sarah Devlin 1841 -
James Devlin 1843 -
John Henry Devlin 1845 -
Mary Ann Devlin 1848 - 1880
William Wallace Thompson 1842 -

Christopher C. Reitze Jr. 1855 - 1907
Elizabeth L. Hoffner 1861 - 1938
Susan R. Reitze 1859 - 1859
Henry Reitze 1861 - 1862
Elizabeth M. Reitze 1863 - 1961
Edward J. Collins 1859 - 1893
Henry Grafe Douglass 1854 - 1932
Charles Archibald Reitze Sr. 1866 - 1893

George Joseph Smith 1857 - 1934
Rose A. Donahue 1856 - 1901
Anna (--?--) 1870 -
Charles Smith Jr. 1858 - 1927
Susan Adelaide Smith 1860 - 1864
Francis "Frank" Smith 1862 - 1916
Amelia Smith 1863 - 1944
Thomas Aloyisius Reilly 1859 - 1941

William "Willie" Thompson 1872 - 1878
Charles "Charley" Thompson 1874 - 1874
Sarah "Sallie" Thompson 1877 - 1877
son Thompson 1880 - 1880

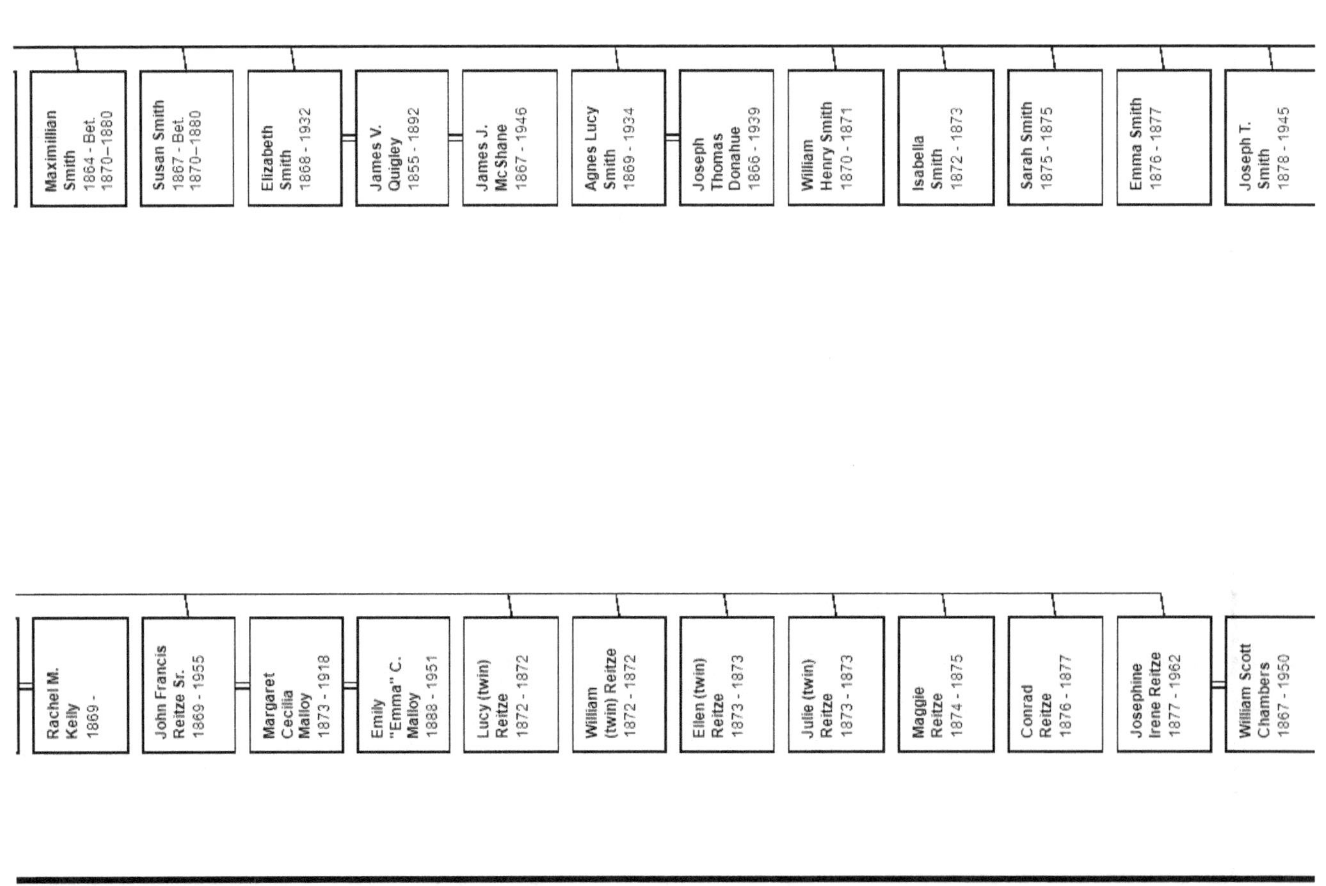

Maximillian Smith 1864 - Bet. 1870-1880
Susan Smith 1867 - Bet. 1870-1880
Elizabeth Smith 1868 - 1932
James V. Quigley 1855 - 1892
James J. McShane 1867 - 1946
Agnes Lucy Smith 1869 - 1934
Joseph Thomas Donahue 1866 - 1939
William Henry Smith 1870 - 1871
Isabella Smith 1872 - 1873
Sarah Smith 1875 - 1875
Emma Smith 1876 - 1877
Joseph T. Smith 1878 - 1945
Rachel M. Kelly 1869 -
John Francis Reitze Sr. 1869 - 1955
Margaret Cecilia Malloy 1873 - 1918
Emily "Emma" C. Malloy 1888 - 1951
Lucy (twin) Reitze 1872 - 1872
William (twin) Reitze 1872 - 1872
Ellen (twin) Reitze 1873 - 1873
Julie (twin) Reitze 1873 - 1873
Maggie Reitze 1874 - 1875
Conrad Reitze 1876 - 1877
Josephine Irene Reitze 1877 - 1962
William Scott Chambers 1867 - 1950

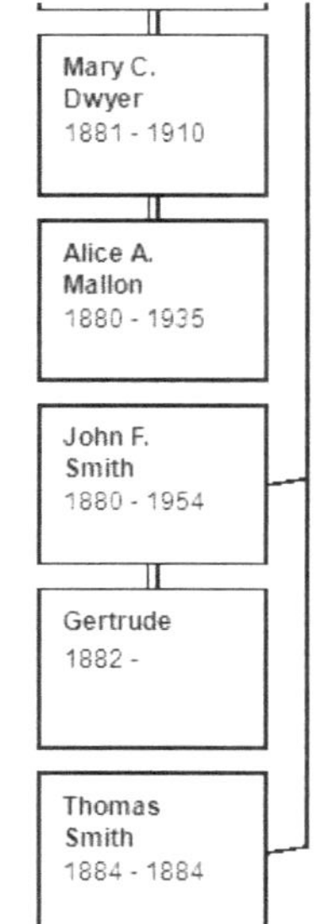

Mary C.
Dwyer
1881 - 1910

Alice A.
Mallon
1880 - 1935

John F.
Smith
1880 - 1954

Gertrude
1882 -

Thomas
Smith
1884 - 1884

The Devlin Family History

Peter Devlin and Susan Kennedy - husband and wife. He was an Irish-Catholic farmer's son who immigrated to Philadelphia during the pre-famine Irish exodus and she was the great-granddaughter of Scots-Irish Presbyterians who settled in Chester County, Pennsylvania, before the Revolution. An unlikely couple? Perhaps, perhaps not.

Despite an auspicious beginning in America, Susan Kennedy's immediate family appears to have fallen on hard times primarily due to the untimely death of her grandfather and her father. Her future husband may have experienced much the same kind of privation in Ireland due to widespread poverty and overpopulation in the northern province of Ulster.

Thus, when Peter Devlin and Susan Kennedy met, ran away, and got married, their financial circumstances may have been such that their ethnic and religious differences seemed of little consequence to them. In the long term, however, Susan Kennedy's marriage to Peter Devlin, which was contrary to the wishes of her parents, created a rift in the family that significantly complicated the process of proving her ancestry.

SUSAN (KENNEDY) DEVLIN'S GREAT-GRANDPARENTS

Susan (Kennedy) Devlin's great-grandparents were William and Susanna (Doak) Kennedy.[1,2]

---

[1]Kathryn Chambers Torpey, *William Kennedy of Chester County Pennsylvania, and His Descendants - A Compiled Genealogy (Including Davis, Smith, Wallace, Russell, and McClure),* (Alexandria, Virginia: Torpey Books, 2014), Chapter 1:1-44.

[2]Two family historians - Joseph Smith Harris, *Record of the Smith Family Descended from John Smith Born 1655 in County Monaghan, Ireland,* (Philadelphia, Pennsylvania: Press of George F. Lasher, 1906), 35 and Edna Letitia Kennedy Haydock. *The Kennedy Family,* (Haddonfield, New Jersey: Edna Haydock, Publisher, 1962), 10 - incorrectly state that William Kennedy was married to a woman named Martha. See Appendix A for a sworn statement dated June 21, 2002, concerning the source of the Kennedy family information contained in these two books.

Although most couples in Colonial American were married by their minister at the home of the bride's parents, it is unclear where William Kennedy and Susanna Doak were married. Their marriage license is dated January 26, 1764.[3]

The marriage register of the First Presbyterian Church in Philadelphia indicates they were married by the Reverend Doctor John Ewing on the same date the license was issued by the Province.[4,5] Reverend Ewing, a native of Nottingham, Cecil County, Maryland, was a graduate of the New London Academy, Chester County, Pennsylvania.[6] He was also Provost of the University of Pennsylvania; and minister of the First Presbyterian Church in Philadelphia.[7]

The First Presbyterian Church, also known as "Old Buttonwood," was originally a frame structure situated in a grove of buttonwood trees at High (now Market) and Bank Streets in Philadelphia.[8] It was, no doubt, an idyllic setting for a wedding, but the church was about thirty-five miles east of West Caln Township in Chester County where the bride and groom were

----

[3]*Pennsylvania Archives, Second Series, Volume II,* "Names of Persons for Whom Marriage Licenses were Issued in the Province of Pennsylvania Prior to 1790", (Harrisburg, Pennsylvania: State Printer, 1890), 73, 141, says:

> Jan. 26, 1764   Susanna Doach (sic) & William Kennedy
> Jan. 26, 1764   William Kennedy & Susanna Doack (sic)

NOTE: Page 73 transcribes the name Doach (sic) and page 141 transcribes the name Doack (sic).

[4]First Presbyterian Church, Philadelphia, Pennsylvania, Church Records, 1701 - 1946, FHL Microfilm Roll 0468374 (item 4).

[5]*Pennsylvania Archives, Second Series, Volume IX,* "Record of Pennsylvania Marriages Prior to 1810: Marriage Record of the First Presbyterian Church of Philadelphia, 1702-1745 1760 - 1803", (Harrisburg, Pennsylvania: State Printer, 1890), 85, 92, says:

> Jan. 26 1764   Kennedy, William and Susannah Doahboth (sic)

[6]James M'Clune, L.L.D, *History of the Presbyterian Church in the Forks of the Brandywine, Chester County, Pennsylvania, (Brandywine Manor Presbyterian Church), From A.D. 1735 to A.D. 1885,* (Philadelphia, Pennsylvania: Lippincott Company, 1885), 233.

[7]Scharf and Westcott, *History of Philadelphia: 1609 - 1884,* 3 volumes (Philadelphia, Pennsylvania: Everts and Company, 1884), II:1265.

[8]Kenneth A. Hammonds, *Historical Directory of Presbyterian Churches and Presbyteries of Greater Philadelphia,* (Philadelphia, Pennsylvania: Presbyterian Historical Society, 1993), 36.

probably living at the time of their marriage. That would have been a considerable distance to travel in 1764 for the purpose of getting married particularly when the Reverend Ewing is known to have visited Chester County on a regular basis during the time period in question.[9]

It is possible that William Kennedy and Susanna Doak obtained a marriage license because they were not personally known by the Reverend John Ewing and/or he was marrying them in a ceremony at a private home in Chester County, Pennsylvania. The Reverend Ewing may have used the date on the marriage license to make the entry in his personal marriage register. The information in his personal register was later incorporated into the church register.

The Early Life of William Kennedy

The early life of William Kennedy is not well documented. He was born about 1736, but the names of his parents and his place of birth are unknown.[10,11]

He is known to have served as a soldier during the French and Indian War, specifically the capture of Fort Duquesne. In July 1758, Brigadier-General John Forbes assembled a large force including 2,700 Pennsylvania Provincials to move against Fort Duquesne.[12] Despite an initial setback, General Forbes had great success. He held a council at Fort Bedford with the Indian tribes of the region, establishing peace between them and the British. When the French realized they would no longer have Indian allies, and knowing their communication with Montreal was cut off with the capture of Fort Frontenac, they quickly abandoned Fort Duquesne, destroying the fort as much as possible. General Forbes occupied the site, which he soon had rebuilt and renamed Fort Pitt, establishing British control of the upper Ohio Valley for the first time.

Among the Pennsylvania Provincials accompanying General Forbes when he moved

---

[9]Joseph Smith Harris, *The Collateral Ancestry of Stephen Harris Born September 4, 1789 and of Marianne Smith Born April 2, 1805*, (Philadelphia, Pennsylvania: Press of George F. Lasher, 1908), 34, documents one such marriage by the Reverend John Ewing on October 2, 1766.

[10]Headstone of William Kennedy, Section 3 N.E. Row 12, Upper Burial Ground, Forks of the Brandywine Presbyterian Church, 1648 Horseshoe Pike, Glenmoore, Pennsylvania 19343-1035 indicates he was 79 years old in 1814. NOTE: This headstone was read on April 11, 2002.

[11]Obituary of William Kennedy, *American Republican*, Downingtown, Pennsylvania, Tuesday, February 22, 1814, Chester County Historical Society, Newspaper Clipping File, 225 North High Street, West Chester, Pennsylvania 19380 says "78th year of his age."

[12]Henry Graham Ashmead, *History of Delaware County*, (Philadelphia, Pennsylvania: L.H. Everts & Co., 1884), Chapter VI:36.

against Fort Duquesne was a company of soldiers enlisted by Captain John Singleton in Chester County, Pennsylvania, between May 1 and May 8, 1758. One of those soldiers was:

Kennedy, William, aged 25, resident of Chester, Pa, weaver[13,14]

The Early Life of Susanna (Doak) Kennedy

Susanna (Doak) Kennedy's early life is better documented. Her parents were Henry and Mary Doak and she was born on March 6, 1742.[15] Although her place of birth is not stated, she was probably born in West Caln Township where her father, Henry Doak, owned a 107 ½ acre plantation that he purchased prior to 1739.[16] The land was located about two miles from the Forks of the Brandywine Presbyterian Church at the intersection of what is today known as Telegraph Road and Davis Road.

Henry Doak died on November 3, 1752, intestate, seized of both real and personal property.[17,18] His widow, Mary Doak, as well as John Jack and James Jack signed an

---

[13]*Pennsylvania Archives, Second Series, Volume II,* "Officers and Soldiers in the Service of the Province of Pennsylvania, 1744-1764: An Account of What Soldiers Captain John Singleton Inlisted (sic) From May the First to May the 8th, 1758", (Harrisburg, Pennsylvania: State Printer, 1890), 474-475.

[14]Audrey E. Bradshaw, compiler, *Pennsylvania Soldiers in the Provincial Services, 1746-1759,* (no place: Audrey E. Bradshaw, 1985), 28. This information was taken from the Pennsylvania Archives, Second Series, Volume 2, company records.

[15]Minors Estate Papers, C & D, 1724 - 1815, Chester County, Pennsylvania, FHL Microfilm Roll 1429176.

[16]Arthur Reid Title Abstract Collection, Brief of Title # 285 Made April 30, 1935, to the Property of William H. Arbuckle & Geula F. Arbuckle (Husband and Wife) Being Conveyed to Henry W. LeBoutillier, Chester County Historical Society Library, 225 North High Street, West Chester, Pennsylvania 19380.

[17]Headstone of Henry Doak, Section 3 N.E. Row 12, Upper Burial Ground, Forks of the Brandywine Presbyterian Church, 1648 Horseshoe Pike, Glenmoore, Pennsylvania 19343-1035. NOTE: This headstone was read on April 11, 2002, at which time it was determined that a large crack in the stone rendered the age at death unreadable.

[18]Estate of Henry Doak, # 1465, December 20, 1752 (filing), November 23, 1754 (final account), Chester County Archives, 610 Westtown Road, Suite 080, P.O. Box 2747, West Chester, Pennsylvania 19380-0990.

Administration Bond to settle Henry Doak's estate.[19,20] Eventually, Henry Doak's daughter, Susanna (Doak) Kennedy, appears to have inherited the 107 ½ acre plantation that belonged to her father.[21]

The Presbyterian Church in the Forks of the Brandywine

William and Susanna (Doak) Kennedy and their children attended the Forks of the Brandywine Presbyterian Church where William Kennedy was, for many years, a Ruling Elder.[22]

During the time their children were growing up, the surrounding community was very rural and many of the customs and habits of the first settlers still prevailed. Members of the church usually arrived on horseback or on foot.[23] A large number of the members attended services dressed in clothing made entirely at home including spinning, weaving, and tailoring. Visits to the city of Philadelphia and beyond were limited. There was no post office nearer than Coatesville or Downingtown and few religious periodicals were available to the congregation.

The Forks of the Brandywine Presbyterian Church played a crucial role in all aspects of

---

[19]The relationship, if any, between Mary Doak and the Jack brothers is unknown, but it is speculated that they might have been her brothers.

[20]Estate of John Jack, # 3659, December 19, 1786 (final settlement date), Chester County Archives, 610 Westtown Road, Suite 080, P.O. Box 2747, West Chester, Pennsylvania 19380-0990 includes a bequest of ten pounds to Susanna (Doak) Kennedy, the wife of William Kennedy.

[21]Deed, William Kennedy et ux to Matthew Stanley, Esq., Chester County, Pennsylvania, Deed Book I-3, Volume 57, Page 236, FHL Microfilm Roll 0555254. The deed, dated August 31, 1812, conveying 10 ½ acres of that property, contains the following sentence:

> ...AND WHEREAS **The said Henry Doak being so thereof seized died Intestate leaving issue one only daughter who survived him** viz. The above named Susanna (now the wife of the above named William Kennedy) to whom the said tract of land with the appurtenances by the Laws of Pennsylvania relating to intestates Estates did descend and come...

[22]James M'Clune, L.L.D., *History of the Presbyterian Church in the Forks of the Brandywine, Chester County, Pennsylvania, (Brandywine Manor Presbyterian Church), From A.D. 1735 to A.D. 1885*, (Philadelphia, Pennsylvania: Lippincott Company, 1885), 107, 134.

[23]James M'Clune, L.L.D., *History of the Presbyterian Church in the Forks of the Brandywine, Chester County, Pennsylvania, (Brandywine Manor Presbyterian Church), From A.D. 1735 to A.D. 1885*, (Philadelphia, Pennsylvania: Lippincott Company, 1885), 32.

the family's life. In addition to being a Ruling Elder of the church, William Kennedy was a pew holder and a subscriber to a fund to build a stone wall around the church graveyard.[24] The few church records that still exist indicate that his daughter, Esther, was baptized in the church and his youngest son, William, attended divinity school at the church which was conducted by the Reverend Nathan Grier.[25,26,27]

And, William Kennedy mentioned the Reverend Nathan Grier twice in his will.[28] First, he stipulated that £100 be paid to the Reverend Nathan Grier on account of a Bond which he was bound to pay the minister for his deceased son, Samuel, and, second, he nominated and appointed the Reverend Nathan Grier a trustee to take care of the dividend of his estate as it pertained to his daughter, Esther.

Revolutionary War Service

The only surviving record of William Kennedy's Revolutionary War service is preserved in the muster roll of the 8th Battalion, First Company, Second Class of the Chester County Militia dated May 10, 1780.[29,30]

---

[24]James M'Clune, L.L.D., *History of the Presbyterian Church in the Forks of the Brandywine, Chester County, Pennsylvania, (Brandywine Manor Presbyterian Church), From A.D. 1735 to A.D. 1885,* (Philadelphia, Pennsylvania: Lippincott Company, 1885), 203, 208.

[25]Forks of the Brandywine Presbyterian Church, Chester County, Pennsylvania, 1761 - 1781, FHL Microfilm Roll 0503559 (item 2).

[26]Rev. J.N.C. Grier, D.D., Pastor, *A Discourse Containing a Short Historical Record of the Church of the Forks of the Brandywine, Chester County, Pennsylvania from the Time of its Organization, A.D., 1735 to January 1st, 1849,* (Philadelphia, Pennsylvania: John Young, Black Horse Alley, 1849), 10, FHL Microfilm Roll 0568855.

[27]A. Wayne Morris, *The Octorara Family of Churches,* (Honey Brook, Pennsylvania: Harold Publishing Company, 1960), p. unk., says the Reverend Nathan Grier was the pastor of the Forks of the Brandywine Presbyterian Church from 1787 to 1814 and that he conducted a divinity school at the church.

[28]Will of William Kennedy, December 28, 1813, January 28, 1814, Will Book K-M, v 10-12 (1797-1817), Chester County, Pennsylvania, FHL Microfilm Roll 0020848. See Appendix B.

[29]*Pennsylvania Archives, Fifth Series, Volume V,* "Associators and Militia - Pennsylvania: Muster Rolls Relating to the Associators and Militia of the County of Chester (a)", (Harrisburg, Pennsylvania: State Printer, 1906), 820-823.

[30]Certificate issued January 11, 1974, by Harry E. Whipkey, Chief, Division of Archives & Manuscripts, Commonwealth of Pennsylvania, Pennsylvania Historical and Museum

The militias were formalized in Pennsylvania in March 1777 when it became apparent that the volunteer Associators, forerunners of the militia since 1775, could not provide the large dependable force that was needed for defense. The militia companies in Pennsylvania were composed of eight classes, each class being called into service in rotation to protect the community.

According to an article that appeared in the *American Republican*:

> In 1777, the Presbyterian Church at Brandywine Manor sent every male member
> of its congregation to the Continental Army. The women harvested the crops.[31]

No doubt, the men who enlisted in the militia from the Presbyterian Church in the Forks of the Brandywine did so at the urging of the Reverend John Carmichael who was known as the "Revolutionary Pastor."[32] Many of those men, including William Kennedy, were assigned to the 8th Battalion of the Chester County Militia. During the Battle of Brandywine which occurred on September 11, 1777, this militia organization was attached to the Light Infantry Brigade under the command of Brigadier-General William Maxwell (N.J.). The battle was short and ended in defeat for the American troops. Although the defeat increased the apprehension and fear of the people in the community, it did not dampen their resolve to persevere in the cause of liberty.

The Oath of Allegiance

A law was passed in Pennsylvania on June 13, 1777, requiring all men over the age of eighteen to sign an Oath of Allegiance.

Commission, P.O. Box 1026, Harrisburg, Pennsylvania 17108 states, "Authority: Military Accounts (Militia), Records of the Comptroller General, at the Division of Archives & Manuscripts. Residence ascribed: West Caln Township." The original certificate is in the possession of Russell V. Kennedy, 1422 Pennsylvania Avenue, Prospect Park, Pennsylvania 19076. See Appendix C.

[31]Newspaper Clipping, *American Republican*, Downingtown, Pennsylvania, Thursday, August 29, 1946, FHL Microfilm Roll 0568856.

[32]Reverend H.H. Kurtz, *Historical Sketch of the Presbyterian Church of the Forks of the Brandywine,* (Honey Brook, Pennsylvania: The Herald, 1944), 7, describes the Reverend Carmichael as being possessed of the traditional Presbyterian hatred of tyranny and a love of freedom which propelled him to cast his lot with the cause of America. When war came, he supported it actively. He preached before Congress, he urged enlistments, he carried supplies to the camps, he counseled with General George Washington, and he threw the whole weight of his great influence into the cause of liberty. His parishioners did the same. FHL Microfilm Roll 0568856.

On October 13, 1777, William Kennedy of West Caln Township took the Oath of Allegiance before justices of Chester County, Pennsylvania.[33] In this oath, he renounced his allegiance to the King of Great Britain and pledged his allegiance to Pennsylvania. The oath he took was probably similar to the following:

> We, the subscribers, do swear or affirm that we renounce and refuse all
> allegiance to George the Third, King of Great Britain, his heirs and successors,
> and that we will be faithful and bear true allegiance to the Commonwealth of
> Pennsylvania, as a free and independent state, and that we will not, at any time,
> do, or cause to be done, any matter of thing that will be prejudicial or injurious
> to the freedom and independence thereof, as declared by Congress, and also, that
> we will discover and make known, to some justice of the peace of the said State,
> all treasons and traitorous conspiracies which we now know, and hereafter shall
> know, to be formed against this or any of the United States of America.[34]

Those who refused to swear allegiance and sign the oath were often subject to confiscation of their property, ostracism by their neighbors, and, occasionally, had to flee for their lives. William Kennedy was not among those who refused to take the Oath of Allegiance.

William Kennedy's Plantation

In 1758, William Kennedy was described as a weaver.[35] In early deeds, he was described as a taylor (sic). In later deeds, he was described as a yeoman and as a farmer. In his estate papers, the inventory included a listing of items that imply he was engaged in farming, animal husbandry, spinning and weaving, tailoring, candle making, and brewing "appel whisky".[36]

Over the years, William Kennedy owned various pieces of property in West Caln Township and Honeybrook Township. Some of his property included the 107 ½ acre plantation

---

[33]Richard T. Williams and Mildred C. Williams, compilers, *Oath of Allegiance, Chester County, Pennsylvania, 1777-1785*, (Newton & Jamison, Pennsylvania: Will-Britt Books, 1987), 41.

[34]The "Usual Oaths" of Allegiance, <<www.mansker.org/history/oaths.html>>, downloaded April 10, 2013.

[35]*Pennsylvania Archives, Second Series, Volume II,* "Officers and Soldiers in the Service of the Province of Pennsylvania, 1744-1764: An Account of What Soldiers Captain John Singleton Inlisted (sic) From May the First to May the 8th, 1758", (Harrisburg, Pennsylvania: State Printer, 1890), 474-475.

[36]Estate of William Kennedy, # 5983, 25 August 1816 (final settlement date), Chester County Archives, 610 Westtown Road, Suite 080, P.O. Box 2747, West Chester, Pennsylvania 19380-0990.

that his wife, Susanna (Doak) Kennedy, inherited from her father, Henry Doak.[37] A second property consisted of a 150 acre plantation that William Kennedy bought in 1787 from the estate of John Jack.[38,39,40] The second plantation was immediately adjacent to the plantation inherited by William Kennedy's wife, Susanna (Doak) Kennedy, from her father, Henry Doak. Some of the property he farmed himself and some he rented out to others. He may have owned additional property in other townships in Chester County, but the records are not sufficiently clear to positively identifying him as the owner. The above two plantations are described, in detail, in an advertisement that appeared in the *Pennsylvania Gazette* on January 2, 1798. The advertisement read as follows:

FOR SALE

TWO valuable plantations, in good repair, pleasantly situated in West Caln township, Chester county, and State of Pennsylvania, 42 miles from Philadelphia, and 4 from the turnpike road.

No. 1 Contains 150 acres of well watered land, with a quantity of excellent meadow, and more may easily be made, a quantity of good wood-land, and plenty of water in every field to give drink to cattle; there are on said premises a large stone-house and barn, both in good repair, and a never failing spring of good water near the door, with the house over it for necessary uses.

No. 2 Contains 108 acres of good land, with a large quantity of good meadow, and more may easily be made, with a sufficient quantity of excellent wood-land; a stream of water runs through the place from one end to the other, sufficient for an oil or fulling-mill, and there is a good seat for

---

[37]Deed, William Kennedy et ux to Matthew Stanley, Esq., Chester County, Pennsylvania, Deed Book I-3, Volume 57, Page 236, FHL Microfilm Roll 0555254. The deed, dated August 31, 1812, conveying 10 ½ acres of that property, contains the following sentence:

...AND WHEREAS **The said Henry Doak being so thereof seized died Intestate leaving issue one only daughter who survived him** viz. The above named Susanna (now the wife of the above named William Kennedy) to whom the said tract of land with the appurtenances by the Laws of Pennsylvania relating to intestates Estates did descend and come...

[38]Estate of John Jack, # 3659, 19 December 1786 (final settlement date), Chester County Archives, 610 Westtown Road, Suite 080, P.O. Box 2747, West Chester, Pennsylvania 19380-0990.

[39]Deed, William Clingan, Esq., Executor of Jno. Jack, dec., to William Kennedy, West Caln Township, Chester County, Pennsylvania, Deed Book B-2, page 407, Microfilm Roll 1047, Pennsylvania State Archives, 350 North Street, Harrisburg, Pennsylvania 17120-0090.

[40]Arthur Reid Title Abstract Collection, Brief of Title # 285 Made 30 April 1935, to the Property of William H. Arbuckle & Geula F. Arbuckle (Husband and Wife) Being Conveyed to Henry W. LeBoutillier, Chester County Historical Society Library, 225 North High Street, West Chester, Pennsylvania 19380.

either; there are on the premises a good house and barn, both in good order, and a never failing spring of water near the door. There is on each of the plantations a large orchard of apple trees, and a great number of peach and pear trees, and other kinds of fruit.

These plantations lie adjoining each other, and will be sold together, or separate, as may best suit the purchaser. The terms will be made easy, and an indisputable title given. For further particulars, enquire of WILLIAM KENNEDY, on the premises, or HENRY KENNEDY, No. 342 North Second street, at the corner of Green street, Philadelphia.

January 2, 1798.[41]

Apparently, the sale of the entire property was not accomplished in 1798 because, after the death of William Kennedy, his plantation consisting of 190 acres in West Caln Township was put up for sale by his executor, Matthew Stanley. An advertisement for the sale of the property appeared in the *American Republican* on October 14, 1814. It read as follows:

PLANTATION

Containing about 190 acres of good land, lying and being in the township of West Caln, and the county of Chester, adjoining lands of John Long, James Neely, Isaac W. Vanleer and others, distant from Philadelphia about 38 miles, about 2 miles from Brandywine Manor meeting house; the same distance from the Downingtown and Harrisburg turnpike road; the Hibernia turnpike is within half a mile of the premises, contiguous to ironworks and mills of various descriptions, with a large proportion of first rate wood land a meadow, a large stone house and barn, new stone milk house over a large never failing spring near the door of the dwelling house, with a room and fire place above the spring; a tenant house, a good bearing orchard of young trees just beginning to bear of (sic) different sorts of fruit. The land would suit well to divide into two tracts, as there is fine springs and streams of running water with wood to divide, and water in most of the fields.[42]

William Kennedy's 190 acre plantation was purchased by his son-in-law, Joshua Davis, the husband of his oldest daughter, Mary Kennedy. The deed was recorded on April 17, 1816.[43]

---

[41]For Sale - Two Valuable Plantations, *Pennsylvania Gazette*, 3 January 1798, Philadelphia, Pennsylvania, <<www.accessible-archives.com>>, downloaded August 4, 2006.

[42]Advertisement for Sale of Property, *American Republican*, Downingtown, Pennsylvania, October 14, 1814, Chester County Historical Society Library, Newspaper Clipping File, 225 North High Street, West Chester, Pennsylvania 19380.

[43]Deed, Matthew Stanley, executor, to Joshua Davis, Chester County, Pennsylvania, Deed Book M-3, Page 204, Chester County Archives, 601 Westtown Road, Suite 080, P.O. Box 2747, West Chester, Pennsylvania 19380-0990.

William Kennedy was attended in his final illness by Doctor Thomas Kennedy.[44,45] Despite Doctor Kennedy's best efforts at providing medical care, William Kennedy died on February 18, 1814. According to the session minutes of the Forks of the Brandywine Presbyterian Church, he died of typhus fever.[46,47] Typhus fever was a deadly contagious disease that took many lives in Chester County including that of the Reverend Nathan Grier, minister of the Forks of the Brandywine Presbyterian Church, and, ultimately, that of Doctor Thomas Kennedy, himself, the only resident physician within the bounds of the Reverend Nathan Grier's charge.

William Kennedy was buried in the Upper Burial Ground of the Forks of the Brandywine Presbyterian Church.[48] His headstone inscription reads as follows:

In
memory of
William Kennedy
who departed this life
February 18, 1814
in the 79th (sic) year of his age.[49]

---

[44]Estate of William Kennedy, # 5983, August 25, 1816 (final settlement date), Chester County Archives, 610 Westtown Road, Suite 080, P.O. Box 2747, West Chester, Pennsylvania 19380-0990 mentions a payment to Doctor Thomas Kennedy for medicine.

[45]Kathryn C. Torpey, *Colonial and Revolutionary Kennedy Families from Southeastern Pennsylvania,* (Alexandria, Virginia: Torpey Books, 2015), Chapter 7:127-130.

[46]Forks of the Brandywine Presbyterian Church Session Minutes, 1822 - 1849, FHL Microfilm Roll 0568856.

[47]Jeanette L. Jerger, MD, *A Medical Miscellany for Genealogists*, (Bowie, Maryland: Heritage Books, 1995), 152, says typhus fever has two forms. The epidemic form was communicated through the bite of the body louse and the endemic form was communicated through the bite of the rat flea. However, it also says typhus was often confused with typhoid fever, a bacterial infection carried by food or drinking water. It is, therefore, unknown exactly what caused the death of William Kennedy.

[48]Letter dated April 4, 2002, from the Church Secretary, Forks of the Brandywine Presbyterian Church, 1648 Horseshoe Pike, Glenmoore, Pennsylvania 19343-1035 regarding Kennedy and Doak burials in the Upper Burial Ground.

[49]Headstone of William Kennedy, Section 3 N.E. Row 12, Upper Burial Ground, Forks of the Brandywine Presbyterian Church, 1648 Horseshoe Pike, Glenmoore, Pennsylvania 19343-

An obituary for William Kennedy appeared in the *American Republican* on February 22, 1814. It read as follows:

> DIED, - In West Caln, on the morning of the 18th inst. Mr. *William Kennedy*, in the *78th* (sic) year of his age.[50]

His wife, Susanna (Doak) Kennedy, died seven years later. To date, no obituary has been found to commemorate her passing. She was buried between her father, Henry Doak, and her husband, William Kennedy, in the Upper Burial Ground of the Forks of the Brandywine Presbyterian Church.[51] Her headstone inscription reads as follows:

> In
> memory of
> Susanna Kennedy
> wife of William Kennedy
> who departed this life
> November 4th 1821
> in the 79th year of her age[52]

The death dates and ages for William and Susanna (Doak) Kennedy are generally consistent with entries written on old yellowed sheets of paper found in the *Kennedy Family Bible* at one time in the possession of the descendants of William Kennedy's middle son, Henry Kennedy, and his wife, Elizabeth (Wallace) Kennedy.[53,54]

1035. NOTE: This headstone was read on April 11, 2002.

[50]Obituary of William Kennedy, *American Republican*, Downingtown, Pennsylvania, Tuesday, February 22, 1814, Chester County Historical Society, Newspaper Clipping File, 225 North High Street, West Chester, Pennsylvania 19380.

[51]Letter dated April 4, 2002, from the Church Secretary, Forks of the Brandywine Presbyterian Church, 1648 Horseshoe Pike, Glenmoore, Pennsylvania 19343-1035 regarding Kennedy and Doak burials in the Upper Burial Ground.

[52]Headstone of Susanna Kennedy, Section 3 N.E. Row 12, Upper Burial Ground, Forks of the Brandywine Presbyterian Church, 1648 Horseshoe Pike, Glenmoore, Pennsylvania 19343-1035. NOTE: This headstone was read on April 11, 2002.

[53]Stephenie H. Tally-Frost, *Family Bible Records*, (Corpus Christi, Texas: Stephenie H. Tally-Frost, 1969), [DAR Library: GEN/VITAL/TAL], Volume II:20 contains a transcription of the *Family Bible of Henry and Elizabeth (Wallace) Kennedy* which says, in part,

> Grandfather William Kennedy d. 18 Feb 1814, age 78
> Grandmother Susan Doak Kennedy d. 7 Dec (sic) 1821, age 79 ½

William Kennedy died testate, seized of both real and personal property. In his will, William Kennedy named Matthew Stanley as his executor.[55] He also appointed the Reverend Nathan Grier and Matthew Stanley as trustees. He left bequests to his wife, Susanna; his children, Mary, Esther, Henry, Susanna, and William; and to the children of his deceased son, Samuel, namely, William, Robert, Joseph, Margaret, Susanna, and Samuel.[56]

In his will, William Kennedy directed that all his property be sold. This was accomplished by his executor, Matthew Stanley, who sold the real estate to Joshua Davis, the son-in-law of William Kennedy and husband of Mary (Kennedy) Davis. The property is described in great detail in the deed of conveyance recorded in Chester County after the death of William Kennedy.[57]

William Kennedy's will also provided for his widow, Susanna (Doak) Kennedy, as follows:

> First I authorize and empower my Executor hereafter named to sell all my lands
> and real Estate either in lots or together as he may think best either at public or

---

(Both buried in Brandywine Churchyard, Chester Co., Pa.)

[54]The *Family Bible of Henry and Elizabeth (Wallace) Kennedy* was transcribed by the late Jean (Burt) Grube, 2020 N.W. 23rd Street, Corvalis, Oregon 97330-1202. Mrs. Grube reported in two e-mails dated February 6, 2001, and February 11, 2001, respectively, that the transcriptions were done more than 25 years earlier when she was very active in genealogy. Then approaching her 81st birthday, Mrs. Grube could not determine from an examination of her files where she obtained the Bible or who presently had the Bible in their possession. See Appendix D.

[55]Joseph Smith Harris, *Record of the Smith Family Descended from John Smith Born 1655 in County Monaghan, Ireland*, (Philadelphia, Pennsylvania: Press of George F. Lasher, 1906), 48, states that Matthew Stanley was a farmer and a man of considerable estate and extended influence in Chester County. He was a General in the War of 1812, an elder of the Forks of the Brandywine Presbyterian Church, a member of the Pennsylvania Assembly in 1829 and 1830, and a Justice of the Peace in Chester County for many years. He was also married to Sarah Cunningham, the niece of Colonel Robert Smith, and was a trusted friend and family advisor.

[56]Will of William Kennedy, December 28, 1813, January 28, 1814, Will Book K-M, v 10-12 (1797-1817), Chester County, Pennsylvania, FHL Microfilm Roll 0020848.

[57]Deed from Matthew Stanley to Joshua Davis, April 27, 1816 (recorded April 30, 1816), Deed Book M-3, p 204-205, Chester County Archives, 610 Westtown Road, Suite 080, P.O. Box 2747, West Chester, Pennsylvania 19380-0990.

private [sale] as soon after my decease as will be convenient and to make a deed or deeds of conveyance to the purchaser or purchasers according to law and to sell all my personal property that is not hereafter willed and my wife do not take and to pay all my just debts and funeral expenses and to divide the residue and remainder as will be hereafter directed.

Imprimis[58] I give and bequeath to my beloved wife Susanna and to her heirs and assigns a certain sum of money being two hundred and fifty Pounds current money of Pennsylvania which is to be paid to me or my heirs Executors or administrators by Joshua Davis at the decease of my wife Susanna by contract and also as much of my personal property as she may think proper and my pugh (sic) in the meeting house...

...and lastly my will is that none of my children or grandchildren do get or receive any of their respective legacies from my Executors until [they] have first given an obligation with approved security if Required to my wife their mother or grandmother as the case may be for the faithful payment of lawful interest to be paid to her annually on their Respective shares or legacies for her support and maintenance during her natural life and at her death to [cease] and be no more...[59]

SUSAN (KENNEDY) DEVLIN'S GRANDPARENTS

Susan (Kennedy) Devlin's grandparents were Samuel and Margaret (Smith) Kennedy.[60]

The Marriage of Samuel Kennedy and Margaret Vaughan Smith

Samuel Kennedy and Margaret Vaughan Smith were probably married about 1790 at the Forks of the Brandywine Presbyterian Church by the Reverend Nathan Grier. Unfortunately, the Reverend Nathan Grier's marriage records for that period of his ministry did not survived.[61]

---

[58]In the first place...

[59]Estate of William Kennedy, # 5983, August 25, 1816 (final settlement date), Chester County Archives, 610 Westtown Road, Suite 080, P.O. Box 2747, West Chester, Pennsylvania 19380-0990.

[60]Kathryn Chambers Torpey, *William Kennedy of Chester County Pennsylvania, and His Descendants - A Compiled Genealogy (Including Davis, Smith, Wallace, Russell, and McClure)*, (Alexandria, Virginia: Torpey Books, 2014), Chapter 2:55-81.

[61]Rev. J.N.C. Grier, D.D., Pastor, *A Discourse, Containing a Short Historical Record of the Church of the Forks of the Brandywine, Chester County, Pennsylvania, PA, from the time of its Organization, A.D. 1735, to January 1st, 1849*, (Philadelphia, Pennsylvania: John Young, Black Horse Alley, 1849), 11, states:

There is no remaining record of marriages or of baptisms during the first ten

Samuel Kennedy was born March 17, 1768, in Chester County. He was the second child and oldest son of William and Susanna (Doak) Kennedy.[62] He married Margaret Vaughan Smith, the daughter of Colonel Robert and Margaret (Vaughan) Smith of Uwchlan Township.[63,64] She was born June 24, 1765.[65]

After their marriage, Samuel and Margaret Vaughan (Smith) Kennedy appear to have spent the next twelve years in Chester County. They were the parents of at least six children, William, Robert Joseph, Margaret, Susan, and Samuel. Samuel Kennedy and his six children are remembered in his father's will as follows:

> Item I give and bequeath unto the Children of my son Samuel Kennedy deceased 100 pounds less than one full equal sixth part of my Estate. I allow the aforesaid hundred pounds to be deducted [of] on account of a certain Bond which I am bound to pay the Reverend Nathan Grier for my son Samuel Kennedy deceased and the remainder of their dividend to be divided as follows: My Will is that Samuel's son William do get 50 pounds more than any one of the other children of my son Samuel and the remainder to be divided between William, Robert, Joseph, Margaret, Susanna (sic), and Samuel or to their Legal Representatives share and share alike.[66]

---

years of his [Nathan Grier's] ministry, and none, of the number of persons admitted to the communion of the church until the year 1803.

[62]Joseph Smith Harris, *Record of the Smith Family Descended from John Smith Born 1655 in County Monaghan, Ireland*, (Philadelphia, Philadelphia: Press of George F. Lasher, 1906), 35.

[63]Joseph Smith Harris, *Record of the Smith Family Descended from John Smith Born 1655 in County Monaghan, Ireland*, (Philadelphia, Pennsylvania: Press of George F. Lasher, 1906), 27.

[64]John W. Jordan, editor, *Colonial and Revolutionary Families of Pennsylvania - Genealogical and Personal Memories*, (Baltimore, Maryland: Genealogical Publishing Company, 1978), Volume II:913.

[65]Joseph Smith Harris, *Record of the Smith Family Descended from John Smith Born 1655 in County Monoghan, Ireland* (Philadelphia, Pennsylvania: George F. Lasher, 1906), 27 says she was born June 24, 1765.

[66]Will of William Kennedy, December 28, 1813, January 28, 1814, Will Book K-M, v 10-12 (1797-1817), Chester County, Pennsylvania, FHL Microfilm Roll 0020848.

All of the children of Samuel and Margaret Vaughan (Smith) Kennedy except Samuel, the youngest, are believed to have been born in Chester County. And, all but their youngest child were probably baptized at the Forks of the Brandywine Presbyterian Church by the Reverend Nathan Grier. Unfortunately, the Reverend Nathan Grier's baptismal records for that period of his ministry did not survived.[67]

On February 5, 1799, Samuel and Margaret Vaughan (Smith) Kennedy purchased thirty acres of land in West Nantmeal Township. The northern boundary of the land ran for 62 perches along the north side of Brandywine Creek and included the privilege of the water and a water born (sic) mill or grist mill. They sold the land on April 15, 1802, to Isaac Van Leer, William Van Leer, and Bernard Van Leer for one thousand and seventy five pounds lawful money of the Commonwealth of Pennsylvania.[68,69]

Operating an Inn in Philadelphia

Samuel Kennedy and his family are believed to have arrived in Philadelphia in 1802. According to several newspaper notices, he was the proprietor of the Black Horse inn on Market Street also known as High Street.[70,71] He seems to have taken over as proprietor of the Black

---

[67]Rev. J.N.C. Grier, D.D., Pastor, *A Discourse, Containing a Short Historical Record of the Church of the Forks of the Brandywine, Chester County, Pennsylvania, PA, from the time of its Organization, A.D. 1735, to January 1st, 1849*, (Philadelphia, Pennsylvania: John Young, Black Horse Alley, 1849), 11, states:

> There is no remaining record of marriages or of baptisms during the first ten
> years of his [Nathan Grier's] ministry, and none of the number of persons
> admitted to the communion of the church until the year 1803.

[68]Deed, Samuel Kennedy et ux to Isaac Van Leer et al, Chester County, Pennsylvania Deed Book W-2, Volume 45 (1802 - 1805), Page 149, FHL Microfilm Roll 0020871.

[69]Joseph Smith Harris, *Record of the Smith Family Descended from John Smith Born 1655 in County Monaghan, Ireland*, (Philadelphia, Pennsylvania: Press of George F. Lasher, 1906), 35, says Samuel Kennedy owned in early life a farm and a saw mill in the Pickering Valley (sic) and that he exchanged his property for the Black Bear (sic) hotel on Minor street below Fifth street in Philadelphia where he spent the rest of his life. NOTE: The reference to the Pickering Valley may be in error. The Pickering Valley appears to lie within the drainage area of Pickering Creek which is near Valley Forge whereas Samuel Kennedy's farm and saw mill were in the area of West Nantmeal Township. The reference to Samuel Kennedy being the proprietor of the Black Bear hotel is in error. Samuel Kennedy was actually the proprietor of the Black Horse inn which was about a block away from the Black Bear hotel.

[70]Advertisement, *Aurora General Advertiser*, Philadelphia, Pennsylvania, Monday, October 3, 1803, <<www.genealogybank.com>>, downloaded May 25, 2007, says:

Horse inn from his younger brother, Henry Kennedy, who was listed in the Philadelphia city directories as the innkeeper from 1800 to 1802.[72] Samuel Kennedy was listed as the innkeeper in 1803 and from 1805 to 1807.[73] The Black Horse inn was physically located at 171 High Street

---

> At the sign of the Black Horse in Market Street on the night of the twenty fourth of this instant A dark bay horse, blind of both eyes, about sixteen hands high, supposed to be seven years old, and has been cried through the market two successive days, the owner is requested to come, prove his property, pay charges and take him away in ten days from this date, or else he will be sold to pay his keeping.
>
> SAMUEL KENNEDY

October 1

[71]Advertisement, *Aurora General Advertiser*, Philadelphia, Pennsylvania, Monday, June 26, 1806, p 1, <<www.genealogybank.com>>, downloaded May 25, 2007, says;

STOLEN OR STRAYED

From the Stables of Samuel Kennedy's Tavern,
sign of the Black Horse, Market Street

ON the night of Thursday the 19th last, TWO HORSES; one of them a small BAY, between thirteen and fourteen hands high, upwards of 12 years old, has a large blaze on his face extending to his nose, long tail and mane, and if the owner's recollection is right, three white legs; is a little skittish on being handled, trots and canters under the saddle, but is chiefly accustomed to going in harness.

The other is a SORREL, about eight or nine years old, between fourteen and fifteen hands high, mane falls on both sides of his neck, has a large swelling on the lower joint of one of his hind legs, but is not lamed with it, is very tractable and accustomed to saddle and harness.

It is believed that the above horses would return home if they were not confined and it is therefore apprehended that they are stolen and detained - if so, a liberal reward will be given upon information being lodged at the sign of the Black Horse No. 171 Market street, or if they have been taken up straying, their keeping and other expenses will be paid, and the person rewarded for his trouble.

June 24

[72]1800, 1801, 1802 Philadelphia city directories. After 1802, Henry Kennedy was listed in the Philadelphia city directories as the innkeeper at Richardson's Court (1803) and then as the innkeeper at 218 & 220 High Street then known as the White Horse inn (1804 to 1811). The White Horse inn was physically located on the south side of Market Street between 6th and 7th Streets.

[73]1803, 1805, 1806, 1807 Philadelphia city directories.

on the north side of Market Street between Fourth and Fifth Streets at Paradise Alley.[74,75,76]

Remarkably, the sign of the Black Horse is visible in the background of William Birch's etching which captures the formal funeral procession of General George Washington, first President of the United States. The etching captures the view west on High Street from Fourth Street as it appeared on December 26, 1799 when Philadelphia was still the Nation's capital.[77,78]

Serving in the Militia in Philadelphia

Samuel Kennedy and his younger brother, Henry Kennedy, were members of the 84th Regiment of the Philadelphia Militia. At an election held on November 29, 1802 Samuel Kennedy was elected to fill the vacancy of Captain in the Third Company of the 84th Regiment.[79] On July 27, 1807 the members of the Third Company reported to "the house of S. Kennedy, Black Horse, Market Street" to cast their vote for captains, lieutenants, and ensigns of each

---

[74]Black Horse Tavern/Inn, Benson Collection, Philadelphia Architects and Buildings, <<www.philadelphiabuildings.org>>, The Athenaeum of Philadelphia, downloaded May 29, 2007, states that the Black Horse inn was located between 4th and 5th on Market Street at Paradise Alley. The Black Horse inn was a different establishment from the Black Horse tavern which was located at 2nd and Markets Streets on Black Horse Alley.

[75]Joseph Jackson, *Market Street, Philadelphia - The Most Historic Highway in America - Its Merchants and Its Story*, (Philadelphia, Pennsylvania: Patterson & White Company, 1918), 81 states that the Sign of the Black Horse stood on the north side of Market Street, between 4th and 5th Streets on the west side of Paradise Alley. NOTE: In this book, the buildings on Market Street are listed with their original street numbers.

[76]Joseph Jackson, *America's Most Historical Highway - Market Street, Philadelphia*, (Philadelphia & New York: John Wanamaker, 1926), 138 states that in 1801 Henry Kennedy was an innkeeper at 417 (aka 171) Paradise Alley located off High Street between 4th and 5th Streets NOTE: In this book, the buildings on Market Street are listed with their modern street numbers.

[77]Joseph Jackson, *Market Street, Philadelphia - The Most Historic Highway in America - Its Merchants and Its Story*, (Philadelphia, Pennsylvania: Patterson & White Company, 1918), 77.

[78]Etching by William Birch, 1800, *High Street from Country Market Place with the Procession in Commemoration of the Death of General George Washington*, The Library Company of Philadelphia, Philadelphia, Pennsylvania.

[79]84th Regiment, 1800 - 1807 (1 folder), Box 2, Militia Election Returns (1790-1863), Records of the Department of State, Bureau of Commissions, Elections and Legislation, RG-26, Pennsylvania State Archives, 350 North Street, Harrisburg, Pennsylvania 17120-0090.

company.[80] A report dated July 29, 1807 states that Henry Kennedy was elected to fill the vacancy of Captain in the Third Company of the 84th Regiment.[81] Later, after the death of Samuel Kennedy on August 9, 1807, several Regimental Notices of the 84th Regiment of Militia appeared in *Poulson's American Daily Advertiser* that read, in part,

> ... The Court of Appeal under the orders of May last, will meet of the house of Michael Fagan, in Laetitia Court, on Monday the second of November next, at one o'clock, P.M. The place of Captain Samuel Kennedy in the Court of Appeal, is supplied by Captain Henry Kennedy.[82]

The Second Presbyterian Church

On Sundays, Samuel and Margaret Vaughan (Smith) Kennedy and their children attended the Second Presbyterian Church in Philadelphia where they shared pew # 44 with the family of his brother, Henry Kennedy.[83] It was in this church that their youngest son, Samuel, was baptized on March 2, 1805.[84]

The Death of Samuel Kennedy

Having operated the Black Horse inn for about five years, Samuel Kennedy died in

---

[80]Notice, Militia Elections - 84th Regiment. *Aurora General Advertiser*, Philadelphia, Pennsylvania, Saturday, July 25, 1807, <<www.genealogybank.com>>, downloaded May 25, 2007.

[81]84th Regiment, 1800 - 1807 (1 folder), Box 2, Militia Election Returns (1790-1863), Records of the Department of State, Bureau of Commissions, Elections and Legislation, RG-26, Pennsylvania State Archives, 350 North Street, Harrisburg, Pennsylvania 17120-0090.

[82]Regimental Notice, *Poulson's American Daily Advertiser*, Philadelphia, Pennsylvania, Thursday, October 1, 1807; Saturday, October 3, 1807; Saturday, October 17, 1807; Monday, October 19, 1807; Tuesday, October 20, 1807; and Monday, November 2, 1807, <<www.genealogybank.com>>, downloaded May 25, 2007 and December 5, 2012.

[83]Rev. E.R. Beadle, pastor, *The Old and The New. 1743 - 1876. The Second Presbyterian Church of Philadelphia - Its Beginnings and Increase, 1743 - 1875* (Philadelphia, Pennsylvania: James B. Chandler, Printer, 1876), pew plan.

[84]Records of the Second Presbyterian Church, 1745 - 1833, [Ph 3P] and Tombstone Inscriptions of the Second Presbyterian Church [Ph 4P] at the Historical Society of Pennsylvania, Philadelphia, Pennsylvania, item 1, p. 165/166, FHL Microfilm Roll 0387874.

Philadelphia on August 9, 1807.[85] His death certificate read as follows:

Mr. Samuel Kennedy aged 39 years died Aug. 9 1807 of ascetis (sic).[86,87]

According to Edna Letitia Kennedy Haydock:

He [Samuel Kennedy] only lived to be forty and died from a strain. He lifted a wagon
that was too heavy for him, to make room for a carriage on Minor Street.[88]

He was originally buried in the Second Presbyterian Burial Ground at 5th and Arch
Streets.[89] The Sexton's records indicate that the cost of the burial was $2.00 and that the
deceased had both a headstone and a footstone.[90] The inscription read as follows:

In memory of Samuel Kennedy who departed
this life August 9, 1807. Aged 39 years
[4] months, and 30 days.

Say live forever wondrous King
Born to redeem & strong to save
Then ask the monster where's the sting

---

[85]Frances Olcott Allen, "Earliest Burial Records of the Board of Health 1807,"
*Pennsylvania Vital Records From The Pennsylvania Genealogical Magazine and The
Pennsylvania Magazine of History and Biography,* 3 volumes (Baltimore, Maryland:
Genealogical Publishing Company, 1983) III:41.

[86]Philadelphia Cemetery Returns, 1807, (Germ Presby - Univ), Second Presbyterian
Interments for the Week Ending August 15, 1807, Philadelphia, Pennsylvania, FHL Microfilm
Roll 1855029.

[87]Ascites, fluid in the abdominal cavity.

[88]Edna L. Haydock, *The Kennedy Family* (Haddonfield, New Jersey: Edna L. Haydock,
1962), [HSP Library: FA/929.2/K35h/1962],10.

[89]Frances Olcott Allen, "Earliest Burial Records of the Board of Health 1807,"
*Pennsylvania Vital Records From The Pennsylvania Genealogical Magazine and The
Pennsylvania Magazine of History and Biography,* 3 volumes (Baltimore, Maryland:
Genealogical Publishing Company, 1983) III:41.

[90]Second Presbyterian Burial Records, 1785 - 1808, Philadelphia, Pennsylvania, FHL
Microfilm Roll 0505493 states the grave location was:

Range C
1-71   S. Kennedy   Head & Foot

And where's thy victory, boasting grave![91,92]

He was removed to Mount Vernon Cemetery in 1867 where he still rests today.[93]

The Estate of Samuel Kennedy

Samuel Kennedy died intestate. His widow, Margaret Vaughan (Smith) Kennedy, filed a request for Letters of Administration to settle his estate on August 27, 1807.[94] Her brothers, Jonathan Smith, Cashier of the Bank of Pennsylvania, and Joseph Smith, a successful merchant in Philadelphia, signed the bond with her. The probate file includes an inventory of Samuel Kennedy's personal property worth $457.52 including two milch (sic) cows and all stable apparatus as well as the furnishings for the inn, the tavern, and the kitchen. There is no information in the probate file about the final disposition of his estate and there is no indication in the deed indexes that any property was sold by his widow after his death.

A notice concerning the sale of his personal property appeared in *Poulson's American Daily Advertiser* on September 15, 1807. It read as follows:

Sales of Furniture, &c.
AT AUCTION
On Wednesday next, the 16th instant, at 10 o'clock
in Market street, between Fourth and Fifth
streets, Sign of the Black Horse
WILL BE SOLD,
SUNDRY articles of Household Goods and Kit-
chen Furniture, &c, belonging to the estate of
the late Samuel Kennedy, deceased, viz.
Feather Beds, Bedsteads, and Bedding

---

[91]*Second Presbyterian Church, Tombstone Inscriptions*, (Philadelphia, Pennsylvania: Historical Society of Philadelphia, 1913), [HSP Library: Ph 3P: 2], 19.

[92]1 Corinthians 15:55, "O death, where is thy sting? O grave, where is thy victory?"

[93]Second Presbyterian Church, Philadelphia, Pennsylvania, Church Records, 1753 - 1914, (Burials 1838 - 1860, Disinterments 1867, Re-interments 1867, Building Committee Minutes 1868 - 1874, Burials 1826 - 1910), FHL Microfilm Roll 0504375 states:

No. Range Second Presbyterian	Name	Re-interred Mt. Vernon Grave	Lot	Case	Stone
9 C	Sam'l. Kennedy	8 Top	K	Small	H & F

[94]Estate of Samuel Kennedy, ADM # 185, 27 August 1807, Philadelphia, Pennsylvania. Register of Wills, Room 180, City Hall, Philadelphia, Pennsylvania 19107.

21

Tables, Chairs, & And Irons
ALSO,
All the Tavern Apparatus, and
a good Milch Cows
For the Administrators,
William Shannon[95]

Margaret Vaughan (Smith) Kennedy, Widow of Samuel

At the time of his death in 1807, Samuel Kennedy left behind a widow and six children ranging in age from three to sixteen. Margaret Vaughan (Smith) Kennedy never remarried. She was, no doubt, assisted in the early years of her widowhood by her brothers, Jonathan Smith and Joseph Smith. She may also have been assisted by her mother, Margaret (Vaughan) Smith, who is said to have spent the latter part of her life in Philadelphia in the household of her son, Joseph Smith, after she, herself, became a widow in 1803.[96]

For several years after the death of Samuel Kennedy, Margaret Vaughan (Smith) Kennedy appears to have continued operating an inn in Philadelphia. In fact, she was listed as an innkeeper at 18 N. 4th Street in the 1810 census schedule.[97]

Margaret Vaughan (Smith) Kennedy was described as a large, powerful woman who was a strict disciplinarian in her family.[98] In the fourteen years after the death of her husband, she successfully raised her family. During that time, she was listed as follows in the Philadelphia city directories:

1808	Kennedy, widow of Samuel innkeeper 18 N. 4th
1809	Kennedy, widow of Samuel innkeeper 18 N. 4th

---

[95]Notice, Sales of Furniture, &c., *Poulson's American Daily Advertiszer*, Philadelphia, Pennsylvania, 15 September 15, 1807, <<www.genealogybank.com>>, downloaded May 25, 2007.

[96]Joseph Smith Harris, *Record of the Smith Family Descended from John Smith Born 1655 in County Monaghan, Ireland*, (Philadelphia, Pennsylvania: Press of George F. Lasher, 1906), 21 says that after 1803 Margaret (Vaughan) Smith lived with her son, Joseph Smith, but she may actually have lived with her daughter, Margaret Vaughan (Smith) Kennedy, or divided her time between both families.

[97]1810 U.S. Census (population), Pennsylvania, Philadelphia County, North Ward, page 174, Household of Margaret Kenedy (sic), National Archives Microfilm Publication M252, Roll 55.

[98]Joseph Smith Harris, *Record of the Smith Family Descended from John Smith Born 1655 in County Monaghan, Ireland*, (Philadelphia, Pennsylvania: Press of George F. Lasher, 1906), 35.

1810	Kennedy, widow of Samuel innkeeper 18 N. 4th
1811	Kennedy, widow of Samuel innkeeper 18 N. 4th
1812	no directory
1813	Kennedy, Margaret boarding house 9 Pear
1814	Kennedy, Margaret 10 Carter's Alley
1815	no directory
1816	Kennedy, Margaret widow 10 Carter's Alley
1817	Kennedy, Margaret widow 10 Carter's Alley
1818	Kennedy, Margaret widow 46 Carter's Alley
	Kennedy, Joseph Smith iron merchant 23 S. Warves d.h. Carter's Alley
1819	Kennedy, Margaret widow d.h. 95 Pine
	Kennedy, Joseph Smith iron merchant 23 S. Warves d.h. 95 Pine
1822	Kennedy, widow of Samuel 32 N. 2nd

On July 24, 1816, Margaret Vaughan (Smith) Kennedy granted a Power of Attorney to her oldest son, William Kennedy, to collect the inheritance due her two youngest children, Susan Kennedy and Samuel Kennedy, both minors, from the estate of their paternal grandfather, William Kennedy.[99] And, on October 17, 1817, she petitioned the Orphans' Court in Philadelphia for the appointment of a guardian for the persons and estates of these same two youngest children. The court appointed her son, Joseph Smith Kennedy, to be the guardian of both his siblings.[100,101]

Less than a month later, on November 10, 1817, Joseph Smith Kennedy succeeded his uncle, Joseph Smith, as the agent for sale of iron from Joanna Furnace a Smith family enterprise in Berks County.[102] His store, American Bar Iron, was located at 23 South Warves at the corner of Chestnut Street. He was also involved with his uncle in several successful business ventures including their investment in the *China Packet* which returned to Philadelphia from Canton

---

[99]Letter of Attorney, Margaret Kennedy to William D. Kennedy, July 24, 1816, Philadelphia, Pennsylvania, Letters of Attorney, C-3, p 104, Chester County Archives, 601 Westtown Road, Suite 080, P.O. Box 2747, West Chester, Pennsylvania, 19380-0990.

[100]Petition of Margaret Kennedy for Guardians for her Children, October 17, 1817, Orphans' Court Estate Papers, v 26, (p 255-301), Philadelphia County, Pennsylvania, Orphans' Court Records 1719-1856 ; Index 1719-1938, FHL Microfilm Roll 1293555.

[101]Docket Entry, October 1817 Term, Orphans' Court Dockets, v 24-26, 1811-1818, Philadelphia County, Pennsylvania, Orphans' Court Records 1719-1856 ; Index 1719-1938, FHL Microfilm Roll 0021850.

[102]Notice, *Poulson's American Daily Adveriser*, Philadelphia, Pennsylvania, Monday, November 10, 1817, <<www.genealogybank.com>>, downloaded June 3, 2007.

on March 31, 1819, laden with valuable cargo from China.[103]

Undoubtedly, Margaret Vaughan (Smith) Kennedy felt blessed. Life was stable. Then tragedy struck twice in close succession. First, on March 18 (sic), 1820, Joseph Smith Kennedy lost his life aboard the *Renown* after its arrival in Cape Henry, Haiti.[104] According to Harris:

> Joseph Smith Kennedy was supercargo of the "Renown" (Cap. Tibbetts
> commanding), one of his uncle Joseph Smith's vessels. The vessel reached Cape
> Henry, Hayti (sic), March 8 (sic), 1820, with a cargo of provisions, medicine,
> etc. Kennedy died soon after of brain fever, after a sickness of four days.[105]

Following the tragic loss of her son, Margaret Vaughan (Smith) Kennedy was enumerated in the 1820 census as the head of a ten person household likely including her mother, Margaret (Vaughan) Smith, several other family members, some boarders, and a servant.[106,107] Thus, at 55 years of age, she was probably once again in charge of running a boardinghouse to make ends meet. To make matters worse, on March 18, 1822, two years to the day after she lost her son, Margaret Vaughan (Smith) Kennedy's mother died.[108] No doubt, March 18 was forever after a very painful day for Margaret Vaughan (Smith) Kennedy.

---

[103] Jean Gordon Lee, *Philadelphians and The China Trade, 1784 - 1844*, (Philadelphia, Pennsylvania: University of Pennsylvania Press, 1984), 144-146 contains pictures of various carved ivory objects from China that once belonging to the Smith and Kennedy families.

[104] Joseph Smith Harris, *Record of the Smith Family Descended from John Smith Born 1655 in County Monaghan, Ireland*, (Philadelphia, Pennsylvania: Press of George F. Lasher, 1906), 51 says Joseph Smith Kennedy died March 18 (sic), 1820.

[105] Joseph Smith Harris, *Record of the Smith Family Descended from John Smith Born 1655 in County Monaghan, Ireland*, (Philadelphia, Pennsylvania: Press of George F. Lasher, 1906), 63 says Joseph Smith Kennedy died soon after March 8, 1820 after a sickness of 4 days.

[106] 1820 U.S. Census (population), Pennsylvania, Philadelphia County, High Street Ward, page 240, Household of Margt. Kennedy, National Archives Microfilm Publication M33, Roll 108.

[107] Joseph Smith Harris, *Record of the Smith Family Descended from John Smith Born 1655 in County Monaghan, Ireland*, (Philadelphia, Pennsylvania: Press of George F. Lasher, 1906), 21 says that after 1803 Margaret (Vaughan) Smith lived with her son, Joseph Smith, but she may actually have lived with her daughter, Margaret Vaughan (Smith) Kennedy, or divided her time between both families.

[108] Joseph Smith Harris, *Record of the Smith Family Descended from John Smith Born 1655 in County Monaghan, Ireland*, (Philadelphia, Pennsylvania: Press of George F. Lasher, 1906), 20-21 says Margaret (Vaughan) Smith died on March 18, 1822.

Margaret Vaughan (Smith) Kennedy was not listed in the Philadelphia city directories after 1822. Harris reports that she "returned to live in the country with one of her children."[109] All of her surviving children are accounted for except Robert Smith Kennedy who disappeared from the Philadelphia city directories after 1824. Margaret Vaughan (Smith) Kennedy is presumed to have "returned to the county" with her son, Robert Smith Kennedy, and his family.

The sojourn of Margaret Vaughan (Smith) Kennedy in the "country" appears to have been short lived or seasonal. In 1830, she seems to have been enumerated living in Philadelphia in the household of her son-in-law, James Coleman, the husband of her daughter Margaret (Kennedy) Coleman.[110] In 1840, she seems to have been enumerated living in Philadelphia in the household of her son-in-law, John Parker, the husband of her daughter Susan (Kennedy) Parker.[111] Between those dates, she appears to have lived for a brief period of time with her granddaughter, Susan (Kennedy) Devlin, the wife of Peter Devlin and daughter of Robert Smith Kennedy, where she was listed in the Philadelphia city directories as follows:

    1840   Kennedy, Mrs. Margaret Rose ab Shippen L.
    1841   Kennedy, Mrs. Margaret Rose ab Shippen L.
    1841   Devlin, Peter weaver Shippen Lane & Rose[112]

This is consistent with family legend that Margaret Vaughan (Smith) Kennedy lived with her granddaughter, when Susan (Kennedy) Devlin's oldest daughters were youngsters.

Margaret Vaughan (Smith) Kennedy died of paralysis on July 14, 1847.[113] Her obituary appeared in the *Philadelphia Public Ledger* on July 15, 1847. It read as follows:

> On Wednesday, 14th inst. after a protracted illness. MRS. MARGARET
> KENNEDY, relict of Samuel Kennedy, in the 83rd (sic) year of her age. [West

---

[109]Joseph Smith Harris, *Record of the Smith Family Descended from John Smith Born 1655 in County Monaghan, Ireland*, (Philadelphia, Pennsylvania: Press of George F. Lasher, 1906), 35.

[110]1830 U.S. Census (population), Pennsylvania, Philadelphia County, High Street Ward, page 46, Household of James Coleman, National Archives Microfilm Publication M19, Roll 159.

[111]1840 U.S. Census (population), Pennsylvania, Philadelphia County, Northern Liberties, Ward 2, page 25, Household of John Parker, National Archives Microfilm Publication M704, Roll 485.

[112]1840, 1841 Philadelphia city directories.

[113]Philadelphia Cemetery Returns, Monument Cemetery Interments for the Week Ending July 17, 1847, Philadelphia City Archives, Philadelphia, Pennsylvania, FHL Microfilm Roll 1906537.

Chester papers will please copy.]

Her friends and those of the family, are particularly invited to attend her funeral from the residence of her son-in-law, John Parker, No. 89 North Third Street, on Friday afternoon 16th inst., at 4 o'clock without further notice. To proceed to Monument Cemetery.[114,115,116]

Margaret Vaughan (Smith) Kennedy was interred on July 16, 1847, at Monument Cemetery then located at Broad and Berks Streets in South Philadelphia.[117] On April 26, 1956, she was removed to Lawnview Cemetery where she still rests today.[118]

SUSAN (KENNEDY) DEVLIN'S PARENTS

Susan (Kennedy) Devlin's parents were Robert Smith Kennedy and Elizabeth Lambden.[119]

---

[114]Obituary of Margaret Kennedy, *Philadelphia Public Ledger*, Philadelphia, Pennsylvania, Thursday, July 15, 1847, p. 2, Library of Congress, Washington, D.C.

[115]Obituary of Margaret Kennedy, *American Republican*, Downingtown, Pennsylvania, Tuesday, July 20, 1847, Chester County Historical Society Library, Newspaper Clipping File, 225 North High Street, West Chester, Pennsylvania 19380.

> In Philadelphia, on Wednesday, the 14th inst. after a protracted illness. Mrs.
> MARGARET KENNEDY, relict of Samuel Kennedy, in the 82nd (sic) year of
> her age.

[116]Obituary of Margaret Kennedy, *Village Record*, West Chester, Pennsylvania, Tuesday, July 20, 1847, The Pennsylvania Genealogy Catalog, <<www.accessible-archives.com>>, downloaded January 6, 2018.

> On Wednesday, the 14th instant. after a protracted illness. Mr. (sic)
> MARGARET KENNEDY, relict of Samuel Kennedy, in the 83rd (sic) year of
> her age.

[117]Entry for Margaret Kennedy, Monument Cemetery Interments (by day) 26 September 1837 - 11 July 1849, Genealogical Society of Pennsylvania, Philadelphia, Pennsylvania, Microfilm XX179:1.

[118]Letter dated February 13, 2001, from Karen Crawford, Secretary, Lawnview Cemetery, 500 Huntingdon Pike, Rockledge, Pennsylvania 19046 regarding burials in Susquehanna Lawn, Section 57, Grave 73.

[119]Kathryn Chambers Torpey, *William Kennedy of Chester County Pennsylvania, and His Descendants - A Compiled Genealogy (Including Davis, Smith, Wallace, Russell, and McClure)*, (Alexandria, Virginia: Torpey Books, 2014), Chapter 4:192-203.

Robert Smith Kennedy and Elizabeth Lambden were married under a Baltimore City license dated December 4, 1811.[120] The marriage took place on December 8, 1811. The Reverend George Dashiell, the first rector of St. Peter's Protestant Episcopal Church, officiated.[121] The following announcement of their marriage appeared in the *Baltimore American and Commercial Daily Advertiser*:

> Married on Sunday evening by the Rev. Mr. Dashields (sic), Mr. Robert F. (sic)
> Kennedy, of Philadelphia, to Miss Elizabeth Lambden (sic) of Baltimore.[122]

The Early Years in Philadelphia

After their marriage, the couple is believed to have returned to Philadelphia where Robert Smith Kennedy was listed in the Philadelphia city directories at the following addresses:

1813	Kennedy, Robert stablekeeper 98 N. 5th
1814	Kennedy, Robert stablekeeper 98 N. 5th
1815	no directory
1816	Kennedy, Robert stablekeeper 98 N. 5th
1817	no listing
1818	no listing
1819	Kennedy, Robert carpenter 86 N. 7th

As the son of an innkeeper, Robert Smith Kennedy was, undoubtedly, very familiar with the duties of a stable keeper. He would have been responsible for all aspects of the management of a stable where horses were boarded by their owners and/or for the care of the stables themselves including housing, feeding, grooming, ensuring the horses were shod, saddling, exercising, and generally tending to the health of the horses boarded in the stable. He may have employed stables boys to assist in running the stable. He may also have owned some of the horses and made them available on a rental basis.

---

[120]Baltimore Marriage Licenses, 1777 - 1832, Baltimore, Maryland, FHL Microfilm Roll 0013693.

WHEN GRANTED	NO.	MALES	FEMALES	MINISTER
December 4, 1811	353	Robert S. Kennedy	Elizabeth Lampert (sic)	Dashields (sic)

[121]Edna Agatha Kanely, *Directory of Ministers and the Maryland Churches They Served 1634 - 1990,* 2 volumes, (Westminster, Maryland: Family Line Publications, 1991), Volume I (A-K):160.

[122]Marriage of Robert F. (sic) Kennedy to Elizabeth Lambden (sic), *Baltimore American and Commercial Daily Advertiser*, Tuesday, December 10, 1811, p. 3, Library of Congress, Washington, D.C.

It was during the time Robert Smith Kennedy was working as a stablekeeper that his wife, Elizabeth (Lambden) Kennedy, probably gave birth to at least two of their daughters, the younger being named Susan.[123] No baptismal record has yet been found in Philadelphia for either of these two daughters.[124]

Robert Smith and Elizabeth (Lambden) Kennedy appear to have had at least two more children, a boy and a girl. This belief arises from the fact that four children were enumerated in the 1820 census schedule in what is believed to have been their household. The enumeration was as follows:

SOUTHWARK DISTRICT

Robert Kennaday (sic)
    Free white persons:
        Males: 1 (Under 10)
                        1 (26-45)
        Females   3 (Under 10)
                        1 (26-45)[125]

Robert Smith Kennedy's Legacy from his Grandfather

On April 25, 1816, Matthew Stanley, the executor of William Kennedy's estate, submitted a supplementary account concerning the last will and testament of William Kennedy, late of West Caln Township, Chester County, deceased.[126] In the document, Matthew Stanley reported a payment of $1,099.98½ to the children of Samuel, eldest son of William Kennedy, deceased. Presumably, Robert Smith Kennedy received one-sixth, or about $183.00, of that amount. The legacy from his grandfather would have given him some flexibility in changing his

---

[123]Joseph Smith Harris, *Record of the Smith Family Descended from John Smith Born 1655 in County Monaghan, Ireland*, (Philadelphia, Pennsylvania: George F. Lasher, 1906), 83.

[124]Kathryn C. Torpey, *William Kennedy of Chester County Pennsylvania, and His Descendants - A Compiled Genealogy (Including Davis, Smith, Wallace, Russell, and McClure)*, (Alexandria, Virginia: Torpey Books, 2014), Chapter 4:197.

[125]1820 U.S. Census (population), Pennsylvania, Philadelphia County, Southwark District, page 109, Household of Robert Kennaday (sic), National Archives Microfilm Publication M33, Roll 110.

[126]Estate of William Kennedy, # 5983, August 25, 1816 (final settlement date), Chester County Archives, 610 Westtown Road, Suite 080, P.O. Box 2747, West Chester, Pennsylvania 19380-0990.

residence and/or occupation if he so desired. He seems to have done both.

Working as a Carpenter

According to the Philadelphia city directories, Robert Smith Kennedy began working as a carpenter about 1819.[127] In 1820, the year his younger brother, Joseph Smith Kennedy, died in Haiti, Robert Smith Kennedy moved his family to Southwark District where they resided at 56 George Street.[128] His older brother, William Doak Kennedy, who was also working as a carpenter, lived about two blocks away at 65 Gaskill Street. It may have been William Doak Kennedy who influenced his brother into becoming a carpenter.

Southwark District was located immediately south of the City of Philadelphia, directly on the Delaware River waterfront. The area was marked by large wood yards used for supplying fuel before the days of anthracite coal. It was also known for the sheds and yards of boat builders and mast makers and for the many ship yards that ran all the way down to the United States Navy Yard.

Robert Smith Kennedy may have worked as a carpenter at one of the ship yards in Southwark District. In fact, it is entirely possible that he worked as a carpenter at the United States Navy Yard that was then located at South Front and Federal Streets. It is also possible that it was in Southwark District where Robert Smith Kennedy's family first met the Douglass family as that is where the Douglass family resided during that time period.[129]

In 1823, Robert Smith Kennedy moved his family from Southwark District into the City of Philadelphia where they resided at Perry Street just two blocks east of 13th and Spruce Streets where the Benner family resided during that time period.[130,131] While living on Perry Street, Robert Smith Kennedy continued to work as a carpenter.

Robert Smith Kennedy disappeared from the Philadelphia city directories after 1824. So

---

[127]1819 Philadelphia city directory.

[128]1820, 1821, 1822 Philadelphia city directories.

[129]Kathryn Chambers Torpey, *The Reitze Family in Philadelphia - Descended from Christopher Reitze Born 1824 in Hesse-Cassel, Germany*, (Alexandria, Virginia: Torpey Books, 2017), Appendix F, *The Douglass Family*.

[130]1823, 1824 Philadelphia city directories.

[131]Kathryn Chambers Torpey, *The Reitze Family in Philadelphia - Descended from Christopher Reitze Born 1824 in Hesse-Cassel, Germany*, (Alexandria, Virginia: Torpey Books, 2017), Appendix D, *The Benner Family*.

did his mother, Margaret Vaughan (Smith) Kennedy. Harris reports that Margaret Vaughan (Smith) Kennedy returned to the "country" to live with one of her children.[132] Robert Smith Kennedy is probably the child with whom she removed to the country.

Serving as a Methodist Minister

Harris reports that Robert Smith Kennedy worked as a Methodist minister after leaving Philadelphia.[133] Unfortunately, this account could not be corroborated. This may be because Robert Smith Kennedy was a local pastor or circuit preacher. In that case, he could have been a lay person authorized by the annual conference to assist the itinerant clergy in a given area. While these lay ministers often had the authority to perform marriages as well as other pastoral duties, records were only kept of the names of full time pastors assigned to particular churches.

The Death and Burial of Robert Smith Kennedy

Robert Smith Kennedy died on September 8, 1837, in West Philadelphia. He left no will nor were intestate papers filed on his behalf in either Philadelphia or Chester County. His death certificate states:

> This will certify that Robert S. Kennedy - died of Tetanus - or Locked - jaw - on the morning of Friday - the 8th day of September - about forty five years of age.
>
> West Philadelphia Septem. 8, 1837   John M. Pugh, M.D.[134]

Locked jaw is an acute infectious disease that usually results from a puncture wound that is contaminated by soil, dust or animal excreta containing *C. tetani* bacteria. During the 19th Century, the disease was prevalent in agricultural areas. The prognosis was generally poor with death occurring within ten days of onset. The incubation period could be as short as two days with symptoms appearing three days after the injury. Locked jaw is characterized by painful unremitting muscle contractions of the face and jaw, arched-back rigidity, boardlike abdominal rigidity, and convulsions which cause the skin to turn a bluish color due to lack of oxygen in the blood followed by sudden death from asphyxiation.

---

[132]Joseph Smith Harris, *Record of the Smith Family Descended from John Smith Born 1655 in County Monaghan, Ireland*, (Philadelphia, Pennsylvania: Press of George F. Lasher, 1906), 35.

[133]Joseph Smith Harris, *Record of the Smith Family Descended from John Smith Born 1655 in County Monaghan, Ireland*, (Philadelphia, Pennsylvania: Press of George F. Lasher, 1906), 63.

[134]Philadelphia Cemetery Returns, Francisville Interments for the Week Ending September 9, 1837, Philadelphia City Archives, Philadelphia, Pennsylvania, FHL Microfilm Roll 1905519.

Robert Smith Kennedy's death is consistent with family legend that an ancestor died of locked jaw after stepping on a nail.

His obituary appeared in the *American Sentinel* as follows:

> On Friday morning, ROBERT S. KENNEDY, after a short and painful illness in the 45th year of his age.[135]

Robert Smith Kennedy was laid to rest in Francisville. While it is unclear where Francisville was located it is thought to refer to a burial ground operated by the Board of Health known as The Vineyard which was then located adjacent to the Francisville neighborhood of Philadelphia.[136,137]

After the death of Robert Smith Kennedy, his widow, Elizabeth (Lambden) Kennedy is said to have married a man named "Allen from Blackwood."[138] To date, no trace of his widow and her second husband has been found.

---

[135]Obituary of Robert S. Kennedy, *American Sentinel*, Philadelphia, Pennsylvania, Monday, September 11, 1837, p. 2, Library of Congress, Washington, D.C.

[136]Appendix A, *Potter's Field and Almshouse Cemeteries in Philadelphia*, says: "Potter's Field 6 ["The Vineyard"]: vicinity of the intersection of N. 20th, Parrish, and Poplar Streets, adjacent to the Francisville neighborhood (exact boundaries unknown); circa 1818–1860 (Library Company of Philadelphia 2010; *Philadelphia Inquirer*, June 16, 1857). Cemetery partially intact. Graves were removed by the city in 1861 (*Public Ledger*, December 30, 1861), but evidently many were missed. Workmen uncovered human remains at 20th and Parrish Streets in 1890 (*Philadelphia Inquirer*, September 9, 1890); more skeletal remains were found below a sidewalk at 802 N. 20th Street in 1895 (*Philadelphia Inquirer*, September 15, 1895); and seven intact graves were exposed in a basement in the 800 block of 20th Street during house repairs in 2009 (Gambardello 2009)," <<www.phila.gov>>, downloaded February 3, 2018.

[137]*Francisville Burial Ground - Lot Holder's Book 1832-1853. (Philadelphia, Pennsylvania: Genealogical Society of Pennsylvania, c 2001)*, F.158.61 F7 contains a copy of the original Book of Daniel B. Grove and an alphabetical index compiled by volunteers at the Genealogical Society of Pennsylvania concerning another Francisville for which a lot holders' book exists covering the period 1832 to 1853. This book was reviewed on October 25, 2006 at the Genealogical Society of Pennsylvania. There were no Kennedys included in the list of lot holders or the list of strangers buried in this Francisville burial ground.

[138]Interview in March, 1995, with the late William Scott Chambers, 9221 West Broward Boulevard, # 2510, Plantation, Florida 33324 and the late Josephine Thompson Marshall, 121 Reillywood Avenue, Haddonfield, New Jersey 08033-2201.

Over a year prior to the death of her father, Susan Kennedy is said to have run away with and married Peter Devlin, an Irish-Catholic immigrant. According to family legend, Susan Kennedy's parents disapproved of her marriage and disowned her.

The Origins of Peter Devlin

Although the exact origin of Peter Devlin is unknown, he was probably born into an Irish-Catholic farming family about 1810 somewhere in the North of Ireland in the ancient Celtic kingdom of Ulster.

As best can be determined, daily life for Peter Devlin, his parents, and his siblings must have been difficult in the early part of the 19th Century. His family probably lived in a modest, sod-roofed cottage with an earthen floor and a single fireplace used for cooking and heating. As was the custom at that time, his father probably rented a small parcel of farmland from an English landlord.

By the time Peter Devlin was born, Ireland's population was soaring due to lower infant mortality rates and widespread smallpox inoculation.[139] This sustained growth in the population resulted in intense competition for farmland between strong farmers who rented large tracts of land and small farmers who were struggling desperately to retain their tiny rented plots. As a result of this struggle, land rents rose to very high levels. The only way a small farmer such as Peter Devlin's father could obtain the additional money he needed to pay the rent was for his wife and children to spin flax at home which he later sold to the linen weavers in the local towns and cities.[140]

Unfortunately for Peter Devlin's family and others like them, by the time he was about 4 years old, the bottom fell out of the rural flax spinning industry thereby reducing his family's income substantially. Given the desperate need for cash, some small farmers began selling everything they produced in excess of the bare minimum that was necessary for subsistence. Gradually, they turned to potatoes, tobacco and whiskey as substitutes for basic food products such as milk, butter, eggs, and pork which they could no longer afford to consume at home.[141]

New means of earning cash also emerged. Some small farmers began distilling whiskey from grain at home and selling it at local markets while others became migratory workers,

---

[139]Kerby A. Miller, *Emigrants and Exiles: Ireland and the Irish Exodus to North America*, (New York: Oxford University Press, 1985), 58.

[140]Miller, 34.

[141]Miller, 34.

leaving their families in the Spring to work as laborers in the agricultural or construction industries both within Ireland and abroad and returning in the Fall with the rent money sewn into their clothing.[142]

To further complicate matters, life in Ireland, both rural and urban, was fraught with violence during this time period. Although some of the violence resulted from individual quarrels and factional fighting between neighbors, the greatest threat to law and order came from secret societies, both Catholic and Protestant. Generally, these secret societies wanted to maintain the socioeconomic status quo between strong farmers and small farmers in the face of an ever expanding competitive market. Sadly, most of their reign of terror, including social pressure, intimidation and violence, was visited on the small farmers who were simply trying to improve their lot in life.[143]

Despite the disorder and the economic hardships, small farmers' sons still pressured their fathers to subdivide the land so they could afford to marry. But, squeezed by falling incomes and rising rents, many small farmers responded by willing their farms to a single son thus forcing the rest of their sons to seek a living elsewhere.[144] In addition to contributing to the disintegration of the family, the effect of these changes on rural Irish-Catholics was that after 1821 the average age of marriage declined and those who did marry had fewer children.[145]

As a result of these factors, Irish-Catholic departures from Ireland began to increase steadily, particularly among small farmers, non-inheriting sons, and artisans in the economically depressed textile districts in Ulster. Even though they were loath to leave their homeland, between 1827 and 1832, Ulster contributed about 50 percent of the Irish-Catholic immigrants to North America.[146] Apparently, in 1834, Peter Devlin evaluated his options and made a decision to join them.

The Departure of Peter Devlin from Ireland

Fortunately for Peter Devlin, passage to America had become less hazardous since 1815. Passengers no longer had to fear impressment by the British Navy or attacks by pirates or French and Spanish privateers. Furthermore, by 1830, most of the sailing ships that carried immigrants to America were built specifically to carry passengers rather than cargo, and technological

---

[142]Miller, 34.

[143]Miller, 61.

[144]Miller, 59.

[145]Miller, 60.

[146]Miller, 197.

improvements had significantly reduced the duration of the Atlantic crossing to only five or six weeks.[147]

On the down-side, the majority of Irish-Catholic immigrants leaving Ireland found it a time of confusion, sorrow, and homesickness. Rather than looking forward to their new life in America, most looked back with tearful longing for the life they were leaving behind.[148] Compounding their personal emotional misery were the deplorable physical conditions on many of the sailing ships including a lack of sanitation, inadequate cooking facilities, stench, noise from screaming children, sexual immorality, drunkenness, quarreling, and general disorder. Contagious diseases such as smallpox, dysentery, cholera, and typhus were also a constant threat particularly to infants, small children, and the elderly. To add insult to injury, many ships carried insufficient water and food of poor quality. All of this despite the fact that the British Parliament had passed numerous Passenger Acts since 1803 designed to regulate emigration and curb abuses including the Act of 1834 which stationed salaried emigration officers at all major ports of departure.[149]

Peter Devlin departed Ireland from the Port of Londonderry abroad the Ship Macedonia. The ship's Master was Captain Joseph Weeks. There were 134 passengers on board.

The Arrival of Peter Devlin in Philadelphia

After about six weeks at sea, suffering alternatively from homesickness, boredom, bad weather, and perhaps a lack of adequate food and water, Peter Devlin arrived in Philadelphia.[150] The date was July 22, 1834.

Upon arrival, Captain Weeks delivered the following sworn report to the Collector of Customs:

> I, Joseph Weeks, do solemnly, sincerely, and truly swear that the report or
> Manifest [words torn away] with my name and now delivered by me to the

---

[147]Miller, 252.

[148]Kathryn Chambers Torpey, *The Chambers Family in Philadelphia - Descended from George Chambers Born c 1815 in Ireland*, (Alexandria, Virginia: Torpey Books, 2016), 1-4, includes information pertaining to the Irish Protestant view of immigration during the same time period.

[149]Miller, 256.

[150]Entry for Peter Devlin; Ship Macedonia Passenger Manifest, July 22, 1834, page 3, line 23; Passenger List of Vessels Arriving at Philadelphia, Pennsylvania 1800-1882; Records of the U.S. Customs Service, Record Group 36, National Archives Microfilm Publication M425, Roll 49.

Collector of the District of Philadelphia [is] to the best of my knowledge and
belief a just and true account of all [the passengers that] were on-board the Ship
Macedonia at the time of her sailing from the Port of Londonderry or which have
been taken on-board at any time since; that I am at present and have been
[during] the Voyage Master of this said Vessel - and I do likewise swear that all
matters [words torn away] in this report or manifest [are] to the best of my
knowledge and belief just and true.

Attached to the report was the official passenger manifest for the Ship Macedonia which
contained the following entry for Peter Devlin:

Name	Age	Birth	Last Place of Settlement	Allegiance	Occupation
Peter Devlin	24	Ireland	Ireland	Great Britain	Farmer

It is unknown who may have met Peter Devlin at the dock or where he went directly after
he disembarked. What is known is that having left behind the rigors of life as the son of a
struggling farmer, Peter Devlin suddenly found himself in a great city where all the principal
streets were paved from the Delaware River to the Schuylkill River and lighted by night with
lamps and gas. The whole city was supplied with pure and wholesome water and there were
omnibuses to carry people from river to river, and railways to connect the northern and the
southern parts of the County of Philadelphia with the heart of the city.[151] Such was the incredible
state of the city. How different from that which he had left behind barely six weeks earlier.

The Marriage of Peter Devlin to Susan Kennedy

What is known about Peter Devlin is that he wasted little time finding a suitable wife.
Thus, the Irish-Catholic farmer's son from Ulster chose for his bride a young woman named
Susan Kennedy who was a native-born American. They were married on May 19, 1835, at the
rectory of St. Augustine's Roman Catholic Church.[152,153] The Reverend N. O'Donnell officiated
at the ceremony.

---

[151]John F. Watson, *Annals of Philadelphia and Pennsylvania in Olden Time; Being a
Collection of Memoirs, Anecdotes, and Incidents of the City and its Inhabitants*, 2 volumes
(Philadelphia, Pennsylvania: Edwin S. Stewart, 1887), 241.

[152]*The Reitze Family Bible - Latin Vulgate Version.* (New York: D. & J. Sadlier,
Publisher, 1844) was in the possession of the late Josephine Thompson Marshall, 121
Reillywood Avenue, Haddonfield, New Jersey 08033-2201. Note: *The Reitze Family Bible* says
the marriage took place on March (sic) 19, 1835 at St. Augustine's Church.

[153]Letter dated November 2, 1995, from Christine Friend, Assistant Archivist,
Philadelphia Archdiocesan Historical Research Center, 100 East Wynnewood Road,
Wynnewood, Pennsylvania 19096-3001.

Their witnesses were Francis and Margaret Rox. Although the relationship of the Rox family to Peter Devlin and Susan Kennedy is unknown, it can be established that in 1840 Francis Rox and his family lived in Kensington just north of St. Augustine's Roman Catholic Church which is located on the northwest corner of 4th and New Streets, between Race and Vine.[154]

The History of St. Augustine's Roman Catholic Church
and the Kensington Riots of 1844

Even as Irish-Catholic immigrants like Peter Devlin were eager to assimilate into American society, they often found it impossible to do in the face of the severe economic depression of 1837 to 1844 and the accompanying Nativism that swept through the city of Philadelphia.[155] The unfortunate consequences of the rift that developed between Irish-Catholic immigrants and native-born Americans during this time period are clearly illustrated by the early history of St. Augustine's Roman Catholic Church and the great Kensington riots of 1844.

St. Augustine's Roman Catholic Church was organized in 1796 from St. Mary's Roman Catholic Church by Fathers Matthew Carr and John Rosseter.[156] The church was established to serve the needs of the ever-growing Irish-Catholic population in Philadelphia. The founding priests belonged to the Brothers of the Order of Hermits of Saint Augustine. They were sent to Philadelphia by the Holy See to purchase land, oversee the construction of the church, and minister to the congregation.

Contributors to the church construction fund included President George Washington, Commodore John Barry (Father of the U.S. Navy), and Thomas Fitzsimmons, one of the signers of the U.S. Constitution. Construction of the church took five years. The cornerstone was laid in September 1796 and the church was completed in 1801. At that time, it was the largest church in Philadelphia and the first church in America of the Order of the Hermits of Saint Augustine. The cupola and tower were added to the church in 1829 and housed the Sister Bell to the Liberty

---

[154]1840 U.S. Census (population), Pennsylvania, Philadelphia County, Kensington District, Ward 3, page 59, Household of Francis Rox, National Archives Microfilm Publication M704, Roll 488.

[155]Kathryn Chambers Torpey, *The Edwards/Scott Family History - Edinburgh to Philadelphia,* (Alexandria, Virginia: Torpey Books, 2016), 16, includes information pertaining to the nativist movement and the American Protestant Association, an anti-Roman Catholic secret society with rituals and degrees whose emphasis was maintaining civil and religious liberties in America and the Bible in the public schools.

[156]History of Olde St. Augustine's Church, <<www.libertynet.org>>, Independence Hall Association, c. 1995, 1996.

Bell.[157]

Soon after its founding, St. Augustine's Roman Catholic Church became a center of educational, musical, and artistic activity in Philadelphia. Paintings by the Renaissance Master Tintoretto as well as the Italian artists Perugino and Carracci hung in the church's interior. The church also boasted a magnificent choir and a school for boys that was founded in 1811 to provide students with "all the advantages of Classical Science with enlightened instruction in our Holy Faith". It also housed the largest theological library in Philadelphia totaling about 3,000 volumes.

Unfortunately, as the Irish-Catholic population in Philadelphia continued to grow, so did tension in the city between the nativists and the Irish-Catholics. By the time Peter Devlin married Susan Kennedy in 1835, nearly half of St. Augustine's parishioners were Irish-born. In fact, by 1840, Philadelphia had the second largest Irish population in the United States. The nativists' fear of foreigners, particularly those of the Catholic faith, was such that they supported stringent immigration and naturalization reform which, if enacted, would have imposed a 25-year residency requirement before citizenship was conferred. Tension between the two groups was further exacerbated in 1842 when Bishop Francis Kendrick petitioned the school board to allow Catholic students in the public schools to use a Catholic version of the Bible rather than the King James version. When the school board acquiesced to this request, a hostile public, all too ready to believe the worst, accused the Catholics of trying to get rid of the Bible in the public schools altogether.

As tensions continued to rise, the nativists held a rally in Kensington on May 3, 1844. The rally was broken-up by the Irish-Catholics. Three days later, on May 6, the nativists held another rally in Kensington which broke-up due to inclement weather. When the nativists took shelter in the Nanny Goat Market, which was considered off-limits by the Irish-Catholics, a melee broke out and shots were fired by the Hibernia Hose Company.[158] In the ensuing brawl, four nativists were killed. Following the fracas in Kensington, the nativists claimed that the Irish-Catholics had desecrated the American flag being defended by one of the nativists who had been killed. Emotions rose to a high level. The next day (May 7) gunfire and chaos erupted again in Kensington which resulted in the death of seven nativists and two Irish-Catholics.

---

[157]In 1752, the Liberty Bell was cast in England by the Whitechapel Foundry. On its initial test ring, the bell cracked. It was given to Pass & Stow, a local foundry in Philadelphia, to recast while a second, identical bell was ordered from the Whitechapel Foundry in England. It is this second bell known as the Sister Bell which hung in St. Augustine's Church from 1829 to 1844. American Bell Association International, Inc., <<https://americanbell.org/>>, downloaded February 5, 2018.

[158]Kathryn Chambers Torpey, *The Edwards/Scott Family History - Edinburgh to Philadelphia*, (Alexandria, Virginia: Torpey Books, 2016), 16, includes information pertaining to the role of the Volunteer Fire Companies in Philadelphia politics.

On May 8, a crowd of nativists set out to attack the Hibernia Hose Company in retaliation for the killings of the nativists on the previous day. A riot ensued in Kensington. St. Michael's Roman Catholic Church at 2nd and Jefferson was burned to the ground along with its school and rectory. A number of homes were also burned and many people fled the area. After completing their work in Kensington, the rioters headed home. Along the way, they crowded around St. Augustine's Roman Catholic Church. The mayor attempted to quell the crowd, but someone entered the church, cut the gas pipe and ignited the interior. The church was quickly engulfed in flames. The entire structure including the cupola and the tower fell along with the Sister Bell. Everything was destroyed except the sacramental registers which were hidden in the furnace to protect them. Without this quick action by the pastor, no church record would be in existence today to prove the marriage of Peter Devlin to Susan Kennedy.

Becoming a Citizen

Despite the unrest in Philadelphia, Peter Devlin was determined to remain in America so, on October 8, 1844, he appeared before the Clerk of the Court of General Quarter Sessions for the City and County of Philadelphia and, being duly sworn according to law, upon his solemn oath declared that:

> [H]e is a Native of Ireland now residing in the City of Philadelphia, aged 35 years, or thereabouts, and that it is BONE FIDE his intention to become a Citizen of the United States, and to renounce forever all allegiance and fidelity to any foreign Prince, Potentate, State or Sovereignty whatever, and particularly the Queen of Great Britain and Ireland of whom he is now a Subject.[159]

Two years later, on October 9, 1846, the record indicates that Peter Devlin appeared before the Prothonotary of the District Court for the City and County of Philadelphia to swear in open court that he renounced his allegiance to the Queen of Great Britain and Ireland and to take the oath prescribed by law to admit him as a citizen of the United States of America.

His petition included the following statement which he signed with his mark:

> I, Peter Devlin do swear, that the contents of my Petition are true; that I will support the Constitution of the United States, and I now renounce and relinquish any title or order of nobility to which I am now, or hereafter may be entitled, and I do absolutely and entirely renounce and abjure all allegiance and fidelity to any foreign Prince, Potentate or Sovereignty whatsoever, and particularly to the Queen of Great Britain and Ireland of whom I was before a

---

[159]Declaration of Intention of Peter Devlin, Court of General Quarter Sessions for the City and County of Philadelphia, October 8, 1844, Philadelphia City Archives, Philadelphia, Pennsylvania.

Subject.[160]

The Birth and Baptism of the Devlin Children

Peter and Susan (Kennedy) Devlin had at least six children. The three oldest Devlin children were Lucy (1836), Isabella (1839), and Sarah ©. 1841). To date, nothing has been found in Catholic church registers concerning their birth and baptism.[161,162]

The youngest three children were James, John Henry, and Mary. All three were baptized at St. Paul's Roman Catholic Church located at 9th and Christian in Moyamensing Township. St. Paul's was opened for services on Sunday, December 17, 1843, when the Reverend Doctor O'Connor preached.[163] It was on that very day that James Devlin was baptized at St. Paul's. His brother, John Henry Devlin was baptized at St. Paul's on November 2, 1845, and his sister, Mary Devlin was baptized there on February 13, 1848.[164]

After whom the Devlin children were named is a mystery. The only clue concerning the names of the children involves Mrs. Ellen Creedon who owned a cemetery plot at New Cathedral Cemetery in which a member of the Devlin family was buried in 1872 and a member of the Reitze family was buried in 1893. Mrs. Creedon's mother was Isabella Sterrett who may have been the daughter of Samuel Sterrett and Mary Denny. The Sterretts had at least three children, John (1800), Isabella (1804), and Sarah (1808), all of whom were baptized at St. Joseph's Roman

---

[160]Petition for Naturalization of Peter Devlin, District Court for the City and County of Philadelphia, October 9, 1846, Philadelphia City Archives, Philadelphia, Pennsylvania.

[161]Letter dated November 2, 1995, from Christine Friend, Assistant Archivist, Philadelphia Archdiocesan Historical Research Center, 100 East Wynnewood Road, Wynnewood, Pennsylvania 19096-3001, concerning the baptism of the Devlin children at St. Augustine, 1837 - 1848.

[162]Letter dated September 30, 1997, from Christine Friend, Assistant Archivist, Philadelphia Archdiocesan Historical Research Center, 100 East Wynnewood Road, Wynnewood, Pennsylvania 19096-3001, concerning the baptism of Lucy and Isabella at St. Augustine, Old St. Mary, Old St. Joseph, Holy Trinity, and St. John the Evangelist, 1835-1840.

[163]Scharf and Westcott, *History of Philadelphia: 1609-1884*, (Philadelphia, Pennsylvania: Everts and Company, 1884), 1391.

[164]Letter dated July 23, 2002, from Christine Friend, Assistant Archivist, Philadelphia Archdiocesan Historical Research Center, 100 East Wynnewood Road, Wynnewood, Pennsylvania 19096-3001, concerning the baptism of the Devlin children at St. Paul, 1843 - 1848; St. Philip Neri, 1841 - 1850; Old St. Mary, 1835-1841; Old St. Joseph, 1835-1850; Holy Trinity, 1836-1841; and St. John the Evangelist, 1835-1842.

Catholic Church.[165] Coincidentally, or perhaps not so coincidentally, Susan (Kennedy) Devlin used the names of these three Sterrett children when she named her own children.

Life in Philadelphia

The City and County of Philadelphia certainly afforded Peter Devlin greater opportunity than he would otherwise have had in Ireland. Although Peter Devlin has not been found in the Philadelphia city directories between 1835 and 1840 nor has he been found in the 1840 census schedule, he was listed repeatedly in the city directories after 1840 at the following addresses:

MOYAMENSING (WARD 3):
1841 Devlin, Peter weaver Shippen Lane & Rose
1843 Develin (sic), Peter weaver Fitzwater above 13th
1844 Develin (sic), Peter weaver Rose & Shippen Lane
1845 Develin (sic), Peter weaver Rose & Shippen Lane
1846 Develin (sic), Peter weaver Rose & Shippen Lane
1847 Develin (sic), Peter weaver Rose & Shippen Lane
1848 Develin (sic), Peter weaver Rose & Shippen Lane
1849 Develin (sic), Peter weaver Rose & Shippen Lane
1850 Devlin, Peter gas pipe layer Rose above 13th
1851 Devlin, Peter gas pipe layer Rose above 13th
1852 Devlin, Peter gas pipe layer Rose above 13th
1853 Devlin, Peter gas pipe layer Rose above 13th

SPRING GARDEN (WARD 15):
1855 Devlin, Peter gardener 23rd Street above Callowhill
1856 Develin (sic), Peter gardener Callowhill Street above 23rd
1857 Develin (sic), Peter gardener Callowhill Street above 23rd
1858 Develin (sic), Peter gardener 2317 Callowhill Street

KENSINGTON (WARD 18):
1860 Devlin, Peter gardener 1222 Crease Street

Based on the listings in the Philadelphia city directories it is apparent that from 1841 until 1853, Peter Devlin and his family lived south of the City of Philadelphia in Moyamensing Township which was located in that part of South Philadelphia known as "the Neck." His wife's grandmother, Margaret Vaughan (Smith) Kennedy, widow of Samuel Kennedy, was listed in the 1840 and 1841 Philadelphia city directories at Rose above Shippen Lane. This is consistent with family legend that she lived with the Devlin family for a short period of time while her two oldest great-granddaughters were youngsters.

When the Devlin family first moved to Moyamensing Township in about 1840 it was

---

[165] *Olde St. Joseph's Roman Catholic Church, Baptisms and Marriages, 1800-1836,* (Philadelphia, Pennsylvania: Historical Society of Pennsylvania, undated), Ph/1C:1-3, p. 557, 638, 716.

rather large, comprising about half of the area south of Cedar Street (now known as South Street) between the Delaware and Schuylkill Rivers. In the beginning, Moyamensing Township was composed primarily of farms which were referred to as "gardens" in order to qualify them for a lower tax rate. Thus, the original inhabitants of Moyamensing Township were not as densely concentrated as were the residents of the City of Philadelphia. This, and the fact that Susan (Kennedy) Devlin grew up nearby on Perry Street, may have initially attracted Peter Devlin and his family to that area.

Unfortunately, this semi-rural scene began to change in January 1843, when about 300 Irish handloom linen weavers walked off the job and marched through their community in Moyamensing Township breaking into the homes of scab weavers to destroy their equipment. Then, in 1848, the boundaries of Moyamensing Township were changed making Moyamensing much smaller, about the size of the City of Philadelphia. A year later, when a cholera epidemic struck the city, many of the dead were from Moyamensing where the Board of Health found "badly located houses, crowded by occupants, filthy and poor, without ventilation or drainage, or receptacles for refuse, or supply of water or the common comforts of life."

By 1850, a large concentration of Irish and African American workers were packed into Moyamensing. Although both groups lived in despicable housing in the same alleys and courtyards of South Philadelphia, they never really shared a community. Violence persisted as each group competed for the most menial jobs and the Irish tried to maintain their hold on political power in South Philadelphia.

The tradition of city street gangs in Philadelphia also trace to Moyamensing where gangs of violent young men and boys roamed. A group called the Killers dominated Moyamensing in the mid-1800s. Some of the gangs were loosely organized groups of thieves and muggers, while others ruled the waterfront, controlling vice and setting fire to the houses of anyone who would not pay protection money. The Moyamensing Killers stole cargo on the Delaware and committed mayhem on the streets of South Philadelphia. The Moyamensing Killers aligned themselves with a volunteer fire brigade called the Moyamensing Hose Company run by an Irish political leader in the 1840s. While these groups could and did save lives, they also forced residents to pay for fire protection and competed with other fire brigades in South Philadelphia. They often set fires and lay in wait to ambush the arriving rival fire company. These fights were not brief scuffles, but riots replete with arson, shooting, and murder. The gangs fought to regulate who lived near them, who socialized at their pubs and taverns, and which fire brigades served the neighborhoods.

Prostitution also made its home in Moyamensing in the 1840s. In fact, there was a directory that listed the bawdy houses south of South Street. One entry described the inhabitants as follows: "...the girls, though few in number, are ugly, vulgar and drunken." A *New York Tribune* reporter wrote in 1848 that there was a "lower and more thorough development of debasement in Philadelphia than New York. The districts - especially of Southwark and Moyamensing - swarm with loafers who, brave only in gangs, herd together. Their names -

Killers, Bouncers, Rats, Stingers, Smashers and others - may be seen written in charcoal on every dead wall, fence or stable door."[166]

It was in Moyamensing Township that Peter Devlin initially pursued his work as a handloom linen weaver, an occupation he probably practiced in Ireland before he emigrated in 1834, and it was in Moyamensing Township where he tried to raise his family. Unfortunately, industrial mechanization rapidly eroded his status and wages as a skilled craftsman so he began working as a gas pipe layer in 1850. It was then that he and his family were enumerated in the 1850 census schedule as follows:

MOYAMENSING, WARD 3

Peter Devlin	40 M	laborer	b. Ireland
James	7 M		b. Pennsylvania
John	4 M		b. Pennsylvania
Susanna	35 F		b. Pennsylvania
Lucy	14 F		b. Pennsylvania
Isabella	11 F		b. Pennsylvania
Sarah	9 F		b. Pennsylvania
Mary	3 F		b. Pennsylvania[167]

Since overbuilding and overcrowding had created a shanty town of ugly and fetid courts and alleys in Moyamensing Township, Peter Devlin decided to move. In 1854, he relocated his family into the Spring Garden District where they resided for about five years at 23rd and Callowhill Streets. Spring Garden District was then one of the most pleasant suburbs of Philadelphia with many gracious dwellings.[168] It was during the time the Devlin family lived in the Spring Garden District that Peter Devlin first began working as a gardener.

The Silhouette of Peter Devlin

According to family legend, Peter Devlin had a silhouette made of himself sometime during his marriage to Susan (Kennedy) Devlin.[169] The silhouette is cut from black paper and

---

[166]Murray Dubin, *South Philadelphia: Mummers, Memories, and the Melrose Diner*, (Philadelphia, Pennsylvania: Temple University Press, 1996), 6-7.

[167]1850 U.S. Census (population), Pennsylvania, Philadelphia County, Moyamensing Ward 3, page 365, Household of Peter Devlin, National Archives Microfilm Publication M432, Roll 809.

[168]Rudolph J. Walther, *Happenings in Ye Olde Philadelphia, 1680 - 1900*, (Philadelphia, Pennsyvania: 1925, reprint: Bedminster, Pennsylvania: Adams Apple Press, 1994), 5.

[169]The silhouette of Peter Devlin was in the possession of the late Josephine Thompson Marshall, 121 Reillywood Avenue, Haddonfield, New Jersey 08033-2201.

affixed to a lighter background.[170] When or where he had it made is unknown, but its reflection of old-time Quaker beliefs is unmistakable. At one time, many Quakers considered it vain and improper to have a portrait drawn or painted. In lieu of a portrait, they sometimes posed for silhouettes. Silhouettes being basically shadows were believed to be natural and entirely seemly.[171] That Peter Devlin would choose to have a silhouette made of himself rather than a portrait is intriguing because his wife, Susan (Kennedy) Devlin, is said to have had as yet unproven Quaker connections.[172]

The Death of Susan (Kennedy) Devlin

On the eve of the Civil War, the Devlin family began to fall apart. According to the *Reitze Family Bible*, Susan (Kennedy) Devlin died on April 4, 1859.[173] This is confirmed by the report of her death submitted by Elizabeth Lye that appears attached to the City of Philadelphia Cemetery Returns for the Week Ending Saturday, April 9, 1859. The report read as follows:

> This is to certify that Susan Devlin died on the 4th of April of Internal Weakness.[174]

Her obituary appeared in the *Philadelphia Public Ledger* on Tuesday, April 5, 1859. It read as follows:

> On the 4th inst., Mrs. SUSAN DEVALAN (sic) in the 44th year of her age.
>
> The relatives and friends of the family are respectfully invited to attend the funeral from her late residence 2317 Callowhill Street on Wednesday afternoon at 2 o'clock. Funeral to proceed to Cathedral Cemetery.[175]

---

[170]See Appendix E, *Silhouette of Peter Devlin.*

[171]Robert H. Wilson, *Philadelphia Quakers, 1681 - 1981*, (Philadelphia, Pennsylvania: Philadelphia Yearly Meeting, c 1981), 86.

[172]See Appendix F. *Quaker Heritage of Susan (Kennedy) Devlin.*

[173]*The Reitze Family Bible - Latin Vulgate Version.* (New York: D. & J. Sadlier, Publisher, 1844) was in the possession of the late Josephine Thompson Marshall, 121 Reillywood Avenue, Haddonfield, New Jersey 08033-2201.

[174]Philadelphia Cemetery Returns, Cathedral Cemetery Interments For the Week Ending April 9, 1859, Philadelphia City Archives, Philadelphia, Pennsylvania.

[175]Obituary of Susan Devalan (sic). *Philadelphia Public Ledger*, Philadelphia, Pennsylvania, Tuesday, April 5, 1859, p. 2, Library of Congress, Washington, D.C.

43

Susan (Kennedy) Devlin was buried on a Wednesday afternoon at Cathedral Cemetery.

She was laid to rest in a plot belonging to Ann Coleman.[176] The relationship of Ann Coleman to Susan (Kennedy) Devlin is unknown. Altogether, twelve people are buried in this plot. Unfortunately, none of them now have a headstone. Despite exhaustive research, the relationship of Susan (Kennedy) Devlin to anyone interred in this plot cannot be established.[177]

According to the records of Cathedral Cemetery, those buried with Susan (Kennedy) Devlin in the plot owned by Ann Coleman include the following persons:

NAME OF DECEASED	AGE	DATE OF BURIAL
Coleman, Mary	50 yrs	May 2, 1853 (Should be April 3, 1853)
Coleman, Catherine	23 yrs	November 20, 1855
Devlin, Susan	44 yrs	May 1, 1859 (Should be April 5, 1859)
Devlin, James	70 yrs	March 27, 1871[178,179]
Devlin, James	72 yrs	April 24, 1872[180]
Coleman, Anna	60 yrs	March 3, 1892
Franssen, Eugene	80 yrs	July 14, 1898
Franssen, Elizabeth	59 yrs	September 13, 1898
Coll, Anna	59 yrs	February 23, 1925
Coll, James	25 days	October 8, 1931
Coleman, Elizabeth	75 yrs	December 10, 1946
Coll, Anne P.	59 yrs	May 14, 1966

---

[176]Report from the Catholic Cemeteries Office, 111 South 38th Street, Philadelphia, Pennsylvania 19104-3179, dated October 5, 1995, concerning the plot owned by Ann Coleman (Section P, Range 5, Lot 21).

[177]See Appendix G, *Memorandum Regarding Burials in Old Cathedral Cemetery in the Plot Belonging to Ann Coleman (Section P, Range 5, Lot 21).*

[178]Pennsylvania Church and Town Records, 1708-1985, documents the burial of James Devlin, 70 years, on March 27, 1871, in Old Cathedral Cemetery (Section P, Range 5, Lot 21), <<www.ancestry.com>>, downloaded August 31, 2013.

[179]Philadelphia Cemetery Returns, Cathedral Cemetery Interments for the Week Ending Saturday, April 1, 1871, Philadelphia City Archives, Philadelphia, Pennsylvania, FHL Microfilm Roll 2020824.

[180]Kathryn Chambers Torpey, *The Reitze Family in Philadelphia - Descended from Christopher Reitze Born 1824 in Hesse-Cassel, Germany,* (Alexandria, Virginia: Torpey Books, 2017), 42-44, documents the burial of the same James Devlin, 72 years, in New Cathedral Cemetery on April 24, 1872, in a plot belonging to Ellen Creedon (Section H, Range 6, Lot 19).

According to a handwritten entry made by Lucy (Devlin) Reitze in the *Reitze Family Bible*, her father, Peter Devlin, died on January 3, 1864, presumably in Philadelphia.[181,182] Despite extensive research in Philadelphia death registers, burial registers, newspaper obituaries, and cemetery returns, no corroborating information about Peter Devlin's date of death or place of burial has been ascertained.[183]

SUSAN (KENNEDY) DEVLIN'S CHILDREN

Life Without Mother - Where Did Everyone Go?

The Devlin family seems to have virtually disappeared after Susan (Kennedy) Devlin died in 1859. After her death, Peter Devlin may have moved from the Spring Garden District to Kensington where he resided at 1222 Crease Street. He was enumerated in the 1860 census schedule as follows:

WARD 18 (KENSINGTON)

Hugh Devlin	64 M W weaver now laborer	b. Ireland
Peter Devlin	50 M W weaver now gardener	b. Ireland[184]

---

[181]*The Reitze Family Bible - Latin Vulgate Version.* (New York: D. & J. Sadlier, Publisher, 1844) was in the possession of the late Josephine Thompson Marshall, 121 Reillywood Avenue, Haddonfield, New Jersey 08033-2201. The entry states:

> My Father
> Mr. Peter Devlin
> Departed this life
> on the 3 of Jenary (sic)
> 1862 [the 2 is overwritten with a 4]

[182]Genealogical chart prepared in the mid-1950s by the late William Scott Chambers, 9221 West Broward Boulevard, # 2510, Plantation, Florida 33324 indicates that Peter Devlin died on March 6, 1864, and that he was buried in Cathedral Cemetery.

[183]Find-A-Grave Memorial # 186212544, Peter Devlin (no headstone photograph), added December 29, 2017, Saint Mary's Catholic Churchyard, Philadelphia, Philadelphia County, Pennsylvania, <<www.findagrave.com>>, contains information about the December 20, 1866, accidental death of a Peter Devlin, aged 60, born in Ireland, who is buried in the "poor ground" at Saint Mary's. He could not be eliminated as the subject of this family history.

[184]1860 U.S. Census (population), Pennsylvania, Philadelphia County, City of Philadelphia, Ward 18, page 410, Household of Hugh Devlin, National Archives Microfilm Publication M653, Roll 1168.

Nothing further is known about Peter Devlin. None of his children were enumerated with him at the time of the 1860 census. What little is known about the Devlin children in their adult lives is contained below.

LUCY DEVLIN. Lucy Devlin married Christopher Reitze on March 3, 1855.[185] Her life is documented in *The Reitze Family in Philadelphia - Descended from Christopher Reitze Born 1824 in Hesse-Cassel, Germany.*[186]

ISABELLA DEVLIN. Isabella Devlin was present as a witness when her sister, Lucy Devlin, married Christopher Reitze at Saint Michael's and Zion Church on March 5, 1855.[187]

Five months later, Isabella Devlin married Charles Smith, aka Charles Schmidt, at Saint Francis Roman Catholic Church.[188]

One of the most fabulous celebrations in the family was probably their 50th wedding anniversary celebration. According to an article that appeared in the *Philadelphia Public Ledger*, the happy couple was married on August 15 (sic), 1855, and celebrated their Golden Wedding Anniversary in the company of more than twenty-five friends and relatives. Those attending included Elizabeth (Reitze) Douglass and Josephine (Reitze) Chambers, and their spouses, daughters of Lucy (Devlin) Reitze.[189]

---

[185]*The Reitze Family Bible - Latin Vulgate Version.* (New York: D. & J. Sadlier, Publisher, 1844) was in the possession of the late Josephine Thompson Marshall, 121 Reillywood Avenue, Haddonfield, New Jersey 08033-2201.

[186]Kathryn Chambers Torpey, *The Reitze Family in Philadelphia - Descended from Christopher Reitze Born 1824 in Hesse-Cassel, Germany*, (Alexandria, Virginia: Torpey Books, 2017), 12-40.

[187]Marriage Record of Christoph Reitze and Lucy Devlin dated March 3, 1855, Saint Michael's and Zion Church, Historic Pennsylvania Church and Town Records, Historical Society of Pennsylvania, Philadelphia, Pennsylvania, <<www.ancestry.com>>, downloaded March 16, 2016.

[188]Notice of Marriage, *Philadelphia Public Ledger*, Philadelphia, Pennsylvania, Tuesday, August 21 1855, p. 2, Library of Congress, Washington, D.C.

> On the 14th of August by Rev. P. Rafferty at St. Francis Church Mr. Charles Smith to Miss Isabella Devlin all of this city.

[189]News Story, *Philadelphia Public Ledger*, Wednesday, Philadelphia, Pennsylvania, August 16, 1905, p. 6, Library of Congress, Washington, D.C.

After more than fifty years of marriage, Charles Smith died on February 16, 1907.[190,191]
Isabella (Devlin) Smith died on February 9, 1911.[192,193] They are both buried in Old Cathedral
Cemetery along with six of their children; three of their grandchildren; their son-in-law, James

---

Anniversary of Their Marriage

Mr. and Mrs. George (sic) Smith celebrated their golden wedding last evening at
their home at 55 North Thirty-eighth street. The house was prettily decorated.
Mr. and Mrs. Smith were married in this city on August 15 (sic), 1855, and have
spent their entire married life here. Mr. Smith was born in Germany, but came to
this country when 20 years of age. Mrs. Smith is the mother of fourteen
children, eight of whom are living.
Their guests included:

Harry Douglass	Mrs. T.H. Oliver
Mrs. Harry Douglass	James Devlin
William Chambers	Mrs. James Devlin
Mrs. William Chambers	Miss Natalie Devlin
John Foley	Joseph McGuire
Mrs. John Foley	Mrs. Joseph McGuire
Joseph Smith	The Misses Foley
Mrs. Joseph Smith	The Misses Donahue
George Smith	Edward McBride
Mrs. George Smith	Charles Donahue
Joseph McShean	Miss Anna Beatty
Mrs. Joseph McShean	Miss Helen Reilly
Miss Quigley	

[190]Death Certificate for Charles F. Smith, February 16, 1907, Philadelphia, Pennsylvania,
5141, Pennsylvania Department of Vital Statistics, New Castle, Pennsylvania.

[191]Obituary of Charles F. Smith, *Philadelphia Inquirer*, Philadelphia, Pennsylvania,
Wednesday, February 20, 1907, p. 7, Library of Congress, Washington, D.C.

SMITH - On February 16, CHARLES F. SMITH, beloved husband of Isabella Smith.
Relatives and friends, also employees of Fulton & Walker Company, invited to attend
funeral, Thursday, 8:30 A.M. from late residence, 212 McAlpin st. (36th and Walnut sts).
Solemn requiem mass St. Ignatius' Church 10 A.M. Interment Cathedral Cemetery.

[192]Death Certificate for Isabella C. Smith, February 9, 1911, Philadelphia, Pennsylvania, #
21264 Pennsylvania Department of Vital Statistics, New Castle, Pennsylvania.

[193]Obituary of Isabella C. Smith, *Philadelphia Inquirer*, Philadelphia, Pennsylvania,
Saturday, February 11, 1911, p 7, Library of Congress, Washington, D.C.

SMITH - On February 9, ISABELLA C. SMITH, wife of the late Charles F. Smith.
Relatives and friends are invited to attend funeral, Monday morning, at 8:30 o'clock,
from her late residence, 212 McAlpin st. (36th and Walnut sts). Solemn high mass at St.
James' Church, at 10 o'clock. Interment Cathedral Cemetery.

Quigley; their nephew, Charles Thompson, the son of Mary Ann (Devlin) Thompson; and two other children in a plot once owned by Sarah Jane Devlin.[194]

SARAH DEVLIN. Nothing is known about Sarah Devlin except that she was born about 1841. She is a complete mystery. The only small clue is a little red speller that may have belonged to her when she was a child.[195] The other possibility is that she may have owned the cemetery plot at Old Cathedral Cemetery where the family of her sister, Isabella (Devlin) Smith, is buried. The theory that she may have been the wife of a man named William Bates has been disproved.[196]

---

[194]Report from the Catholic Cemeteries Office, 111 South 38th Street, Philadelphia, Pennsylvania 19104-3179, dated June 6, 2008, concerning the plot owned by Sarah Jane Devlin at Cathedral Cemetery (Section S, Range 3, Lot 54).

NAME OF DECEASED	AGE	DATE OF BURIAL
Smith, Susan	child	3-10-65 (rem. from M-4-41) daughter
Spence, William McClelland	1yr 1 mo	8-24-70 relationship unknown
Thompson, Charles	6 months	9-16-74 nephew
Donahue, Joseph	1 week	10-15-90 grandson
Reilly, Isabella	3 yrs	1/15/99 granddaughter
Quigley, James	39 yrs	12-21-92 son-in-law
Smith, Joseph	1 yr 6 mos	1-9-07 grandson
Smith, Charles	76 yrs	2-21-07 father
Smith, Isabella	72 yrs	2-13-11 mother
Smith, Sarah	2 days	3-29-75 daughter
Smith, Emma	1 yr 4 mos	11-11-77 daughter
Smith, William Henry	1 yr 4 mos	6-7-71 son
Smith, Isabelle	5-1/2 mos	4-25-73 daughter
Smith, Thomas	1-1/4 mos	6-17-84 son
Rafferty, Annie	8 mos	3-28-07 relationship unknown

[195]The speller was in the possession of the late Josephine Thompson Marshall, 121 Reillywood Avenue, Haddonfield, New Jersey 08033-2201. The book contains the following four handwritten entries: *S. Devlin's own book; Sept 1844; Sarah; and Develin.*

[196]There is a Sarah J. Devlin who married a William Bates on April 9, 1865, at St. Michael's Roman Catholic Church. She died on February 8, 1911, in Philadelphia, but her parents' names were not stated on the certificate. Two people who descend from her were contacted. The first, Rob Risko, said that Sarah (Devlin) Bates was born in Ireland in 1844-1847 and her parents were Peter Devlin and Bridget McGurk. The second, Jean Almond, said that Sarah (Devlin) Bates was born in Ireland in 1844 and her parents were probably Peter and Sarah Devlin. Regrettably, this Sarah Devlin is not the subject of this family history.

JAMES DEVLIN. James Devlin was born December 10, 1843, and baptized on December 17, 1843, at Saint Paul's Roman Catholic Church. His sponsors were James Patterson and Ann Kelly.[197] No further clues have been found about James Devlin except for a stamp in the *Reitze Family Bible* that reads: ***J. Devlin***.[198,199] Directly above the ***J. Devlin*** stamp is another stamp that reads: ***Eugene Devlin***.[200,201,202]

---

[197]Letter dated July 23, 2002, from Christine Friend, Assistant Archivist, Philadelphia Archdiocesan Historical Research Center, 100 East Wynnewood Road, Wynnewood, Pennsylvania 19096-3001 regarding the three youngest children of Peter Devlin and Susan Kennedy that were baptized at St. Paul's Roman Catholic Church.

[198]*The Reitze Family Bible - Latin Vulgate Version*. (New York: D. & J. Sadlier, Publisher, 1844) was in the possession of the late Josephine Thompson Marshall, 121 Reillywood Avenue, Haddonfield, New Jersey 08033-2201.

[199]The names of a Mr. & Mrs. James Devlin and their daughter, Natalie, appeared in a news story published in the *Philadelphia Public Ledger* on Wednesday, August 16, 1905, about the Golden Wedding Anniversary Party of Charles and Isabella (Devlin) Smith. Research reveals that this James Devlin is not the subject of this family history in that his death certificate issued on April 16, 1913, states he was 55 years of age at the time he died and the names of his parents were John Devlin and Ann McWilliams. His wife, Ellen, who died on September 5, 1924, was the daughter of James Lenahan and Margaret Girard. Their daughter, Natalie McGovern, wife of Owen McGovern, died on October 29, 1934. They are all buried in New Cathedral Cemetery.

[200]The relationship of Eugene Devlin to the Devlin family chronicled in this family history is unknown except that he was living at the same address as Lucy (Devlin) Reitze at the time of his death.

[201]Philadelphia Cemetery Returns, Machpelah Cemetery Interments for the Week Ending December 16, 1882, Philadelphia City Archives, Philadelphia, Pennsylvania, 19108 contains a Coroner's Certificate for Eugene Devlin, aged 74 (sic), born in Lancaster, Pennsylvania (sic), living at 3214 Saint James Street (sic), that says he died on December 8, 1882 having been accidentally killed on the Pennsylvania Railroad, 32nd & Markets Streets.

[202]Obituary of Eugene Devlin, *The Times*, Philadelphia, Pennsylvania, Saturday, December 9, 1882, <<www.newspapers.com>>, downloaded April 15, 2018.

> A Railroad Employe (sic) Killed
>
> Eugene Devlin, 69 (sic) years old, employed by
> the Pennsylvania Railroad Company, while wheeling
> a barrel of oil along the tracks in the yard at Thirty-
> second Street Station about 10 o'clock yesterday was
> struck by an express train. He was entangled be-
> tween the handles of the wheelbarrow, thrown

JOHN HENRY DEVLIN. John Henry Devlin was born on October 23, 1845 and baptized on November 2, 1845 at Saint Paul's Roman Catholic Church. His sponsors were Patrick Devlin and Ellen Devlin.[203]

John Henry Devlin was a Civil War veteran. His Civil War Discharge Certificate yields a few clues.[204] According to the discharge certificate, John Henry Devlin was born in Philadelphia and enrolled there on September 3, 1861, to serve three years in Company C, 2nd Pennsylvania Cavalry (59th Regiment). His duties generally involved reconnaissance missions, destroying Confederate railroads and supplies, participating in raids and skirmishes, performing courier services and orderly services, and guarding prisoners.

John Henry Devlin's military service record indicates that in July 1863 he was present with his company during the Battle of Gettysburg where his company was attached to the provost guard at headquarters.[205] After the war was over, John Henry Devlin's name was inscribed on the wall of the Pennsylvania Memorial at Gettysburg. This memorial, which stands on Cemetery Ridge, is a Beaux-Arts colossus. It was dedicated on September 27, 1910, to commemorate the sacrifice of those men from Pennsylvania who participated in the Battle of Gettysburg.

John Henry Devlin was officially discharged on January 15, 1864, at Bealton Station, Virginia, and immediately reenlisted as a Veteran Volunteer. In his discharge certificate John Henry Devlin was described as 18 years of age in 1864, 5 feet 8 inches tall, of dark complexion, black eyes, and dark hair, and by occupation when enrolled, a boatman.[206]

---

under the train and cut in two. The remains were
sent to Undertaker Bair's, on Filbert street. Devlin
resided at 3214 St. James' Place (sic), West Philadelphia.

[203]Letter dated July 23, 2002, from Christine Friend, Assistant Archivist, Philadelphia Archdiocesan Historical Research Center, 100 East Wynnewood Road, Wynnewood, Pennsylvania 19096-3001 regarding the three youngest children of Peter Devlin and Susan Kennedy that were baptized at St. Paul's Roman Catholic Church.

[204]The original Discharge Certificate for John Henry Devlin, Company C, 2nd Pennsylvania Cavalry (59th Regiment) was in the possession of the late William Scott Chambers, 9221 West Broward Boulevard, # 2510, Plantation, Florida 33324.

[205]Union Compiled Military Service Record for John Henry Devlin, Co. C, 2nd Pennsylvania Cavalry (59th Regiment), Records of the Adjutant General's Office, Record Group 94, National Archives, Washington, D.C.

[206]This is in contrast to the description contained in John Henry Devlin's Compiled Military Service Record with the 2nd Pennsylvania Cavalry (59th Regiment) which states that he was *18 years old in 1861*, 5 feet *3 inches* tall, of *light* complexion, *brown* eyes, and dark hair, and by occupation when enrolled, a boatman.

Upon re-enlistment as a Veteran Volunteer, John Henry Devlin was transferred to Company C, 1st Regiment of the Pennsylvania Provisional Cavalry.[207] He served there until June 25, 1865, when for some unexplained reason he deserted for several days. The desertion is mystifying particularly because it occurred more than two months after General Robert E. Lee surrendered the Confederate Army at Appomattox. He was mustered out of the service with his company at St. Cloud's, Virginia, on July 13, 1865.

Nothing more is known about John Henry Devlin except for a notation made on September 12, 1891, in his compiled military service record with the 1st Regiment of the Pennsylvania Provisional Cavalry that says:

> The charge of desertion of June 25, 1865, against this man is removed under the provisions of section 2 of the act of Congress, approved March 2, 1889.
>
> He was absent without leave from June 25, 1865, to July 6, 1865.

Who may have petitioned the government for removal of the charge of desertion against John Henry Devlin is unknown at this time. Also, in relation to this desertion, a cryptic hand-written notation was added in 1893 to the top of John Henry Devlin's original Discharge Certificate. It states:

> Pay and Bounty disallowed by Settlement 157194 February 15 1893
>
> Second Comptroller

No information has been uncovered concerning who may have petitioned the government for back pay and bounty due to John Henry Devlin. Nothing useful was found in the settled military claims at the Pennsylvania State Archives nor was there anything of note in the correspondence of the Record and Pensions Office at the National Archives.[208,209]

---

[207]Union Compiled Military Service Record for John Henry Devlin, Co. C, 1st Regiment of the Pennsylvania Provisional Cavalry, Records of the Adjutant General's Office, Record Group 94, National Archives, Washington, D.C.

[208]Military Claims Settled, 1887 - 1902, Pennsylvania, Auditor General's Office, LDS Family History Library, Salt Lake City, Utah, Microfilm Rolls 1021413, 1021414.

[209]Correspondence Concerning Military Service of John Henry Devlin, (R&P # 260499, November 11, 1890, and R&P # 297220, September 4, 1891), Records of the Record and Pensions Office, Record Group 94, National Archives, Washington, D.C.

Finally, John Henry Devlin could not be located in the 1890 veterans census.[210]

MARY ANN DEVLIN.   Mary Ann Devlin was born on February 4, 1848, and baptized on February 13, 1848, at Saint Paul's Roman Catholic Church. Her sponsors were Michael Mount and Bridget Mount.[211]

After the death of her mother, Mary Ann Devlin appears to have lived with her sister, Isabella (Devlin) Smith with whom she was enumerated in the 1860 census.[212]

On September 5, 1870, Mary Ann Devlin married William Wallace Thompson at the Church of the Redemption.[213] The Church of the Redemption was a Protestant Episcopal church located at 22nd and Callowhill in the Spring Garden District of Philadelphia. Mary Ann Devlin was 22 years old and William Wallace Thompson was about 28 years old at the time of their marriage.[214]

Mary Ann (Devlin) Thompson and her husband had four children - William, Charles, Sarah and an unnamed stillborn son. Tragically, all of their children died between 1872 and 1880 after which Mary Ann (Devlin) Thompson, herself, died on May 31, 1880 at the age of

---

[210]Special Schedule of the Eleventh Census (1890) Enumerating Union Veterans and Widows of Union Veterans of the Civil War, M123, Rolls 78-80, Philadelphia County, Pennsylvania.

[211]Letter dated July 23, 2002, from Christine Friend, Assistant Archivist, Philadelphia Archdiocesan Historical Research Center, 100 East Wynnewood Road, Wynnewood, Pennsylvania 19096-3001 regarding the three youngest children of Peter Devlin and Susan Kennedy that were baptized at St. Paul's Roman Catholic Church.

[212]1860 U.S. Census (population), Pennsylvania, Philadelphia County, City of Philadelphia, Ward 1, page 621, Household of Charles Smith, National Archives Microfilm Publication M653, Roll 1151.

[213]Marriage Record of William Wallace Thompson and Mary Ann Devlin dated September 5, 1870, Church of the Redemption, Historic Pennsylvania Church and Town Records, Historical Society of Pennsylvania, Philadelphia, Pennsylvania, <<www.ancestry.com>>, downloaded February 19, 2018.

[214]Kathryn Chambers Torpey, *The Edwards/Scott Family History - Edinburgh to Philadelphia*, (Alexandria, Virginia: Torpey Books, 2016), 16, 20, 31 documents the marriages of three of the Edwards siblings at the Church of the Redemption, particularly the marriage of Annie Adam Edwards and George Washington Chambers on July 4, 1866.

31.[215] Her obituary appeared in the *Philadelphia Inquirer* on June 2, 1880. It read as follows:

> THOMPSON - On the 31st ult, MARY A. wife of William W. Thompson, aged thirty-one years and four months. The relatives and friends of the family are respectfully invited to attend the funeral, this afternoon, at 2 o'clock from the residence of her husband, No. 1903 Jackson street. Interment at Fernwood Cemetery.[216]

Her son, Charles, is buried in Old Cathedral Cemetery in the same plot as his aunt, Isabella (Devlin) Smith.[217] Mary Ann (Devlin) Thompson and her other three children are buried at Fernwood Cemetery.[218,219,220,221]

Nothing is known about William Wallace Thompson, after the death of his wife.

---

[215]Pennsylvania, Philadelphia City Death Certificates, 1803-1915, FHL Microfilm Roll 2046880, <<www.familysearch.org>>, downloaded February 19, 2018, re: Mary Ann Thompson, d. May 31, 1880, Fernwood Cemetery.

[216]Obituary of Mary A. Thompson, *Philadelphia Inquirer*, Philadelphia, Pennsylvania, Wednesday, June 2, 1880, <<www.newspapers.com>>, downloaded April 15, 2016.

[217]Report from the Catholic Cemeteries Office, 111 South 38th Street, Philadelphia, Pennsylvania 19104-3179, dated June 6, 2008, concerning the plot owned by Sarah Jane Devlin at Cathedral Cemetery (Section S, Range 3, Lot 54).

[218]Burial of Sallie Thompson, Fernwood Cemetery Burial Register, May 1877, Section 27, Lot 207, p 128, Historic Pennsylvania Church and Town Records, Historical Society of Pennsylvania, Philadelphia, Pennsylvania, <<www.ancestry.com>>, downloaded February 19, 2018.

[219]Burial of William Thompson, Fernwood Cemetery Burial Register, August 1878, Section 27, Lot 207, p 164, Historic Pennsylvania Church and Town Records, Historical Society of Pennsylvania, Philadelphia, Pennsylvania, <<www.ancestry.com>>, downloaded February 19, 2018.

[220]Burial of stillborn Thompson, Fernwood Cemetery Burial Register, May 1880, Section 27, Lot 207, p 216, Historic Pennsylvania Church and Town Records, Historical Society of Pennsylvania, Philadelphia, Pennsylvania, <<www.ancestry.com>>, downloaded February 19, 2018.

[221]Burial of Mary A. Thompson, Fernwood Cemetery Burial Register, May 1880, Section 27, Lot 207, p 216, Historic Pennsylvania Church and Town Records, Historical Society of Pennsylvania, Philadelphia, Pennsylvania, <<www.ancestry.com>>, downloaded February 19, 2018.

Source for the Kennedy family information contained in Joseph Smith Harris' family history entitled *Record of the Smith Family Descended from John Smith Born 1655 in County Monaghan, Ireland,* **Philadelphia: Press of John Lasher, 1906**

TO WHOM IT MAY CONCERN:

My great-aunt, Edna Kennedy Haydock, and great-uncle, Charles M.T. Kennedy, told me that my great-grandfather, Samuel Ridgway Kennedy (1847-1936), helped compile the Kennedy information in the *Record of the Smith Family Descended from John Smith Born 1655 in County Monaghan, Ireland,* Press of John Lasher, 1906. My relatives told me he and his *son*, Samuel, gathered the Kennedy information over many years primarily from his father, Samuel William Kennedy (1819-1886), from Bible records, and conversations with other family members, and public records.

My great-grandfather was the cousin of Joseph Smith Harris (1836-1910). They were also personal friends, and they shared an avid interest in preserving the family history. It was common knowledge in my family that my great-grandfather and Joseph Smith Harris worked together to prepare the Kennedy narratives and charts that appear in the book.

Russell Vance Kennedy
1422 Pennsylvania Avenue
Prospect Park, PA 19076-1108

State of Pennsylvania
County of Delaware

Personally appeared before me Russell Vance Kennedy, signer of the above statement, who made an oath before me that the statement therein contained is true to the best of his knowledge and belief.

Sworn and subscribed before me this *21* day of *JUNE*, 2002.

Notary Public

Notarial Seal
John Sloan, Notary Public
Ridley Twp., Delaware County
My Commission Expires May 10, 2004
Member, Pennsylvania Association of Notaries

Appendix A

Will of William Kennedy, December 28, 1813, February 28, 1814, Will Book K-M, v 10-12 (1797-1817), Chester County, Pennsylvania, LDS Family History Library, Salt Lake City, Utah, Microfilm Roll 0020848.

Will of William Kennedy

In the name of God Amen I William Kennedy of West Caln township in the county of Chester and the state of Pennsylvania being far advanced in years but of sound mind and memory thanks be given to God for the same calling to mind the mortality of my body and knowing that it is appointed for all men once to die I do make and ordain this my last will and testament that is to say first of all I give and recommend my soul into the hands of God that gave it and my body to the Earth to be buried in a decent Christian-like manner and as concerning such worldly Estate as it hath pleased God to bless me with in this life I give and dispose of the same as follows:

First I authorize and empower my Executor hereafter named to sell all my lands and real Estate either in lots or together as he may think best either at public or private [sale] as soon after my decease as will be convenient and to make a deed or deeds of conveyance to the purchaser or purchasers according to law and to sell all my personal property that is not hereafter willed and my wife do not take and to pay all my just debts and funeral expenses and to divide the residue and remainder as will be hereafter directed.

Inprimiss I give and bequeath to my beloved wife Susanna and to her heirs and assigns a certain sum of money being two hundred and fifty pounds current money of Pennsylvania which is to be paid to me or my heirs Executors or administrators by Joshua Davis at the decease of my wife Susanna by contract and also as much of my personal property as she may think proper and my [pew] in the meeting house and to take and give my Daughter Susanna as much of my personal property and household goods as will make her equal with my other Daughters that is married.

Item I give and bequeath unto my daughter Mary Davis and to her heirs and assigns one full equal sixth part of my Estate after my debts and specific legacies is all paid.

Item I give and bequeath unto the Children of my son Samuel Kennedy deceased one hundred pounds less than one full equal sixth part of my Estate. I allow the aforesaid hundred pounds to be deducted [off] on account of a certain Bond which I am bound to pay the Reverend Nathan Greer for my son Samuel Kennedy deceased and the remainder of their dividend to be divided as follows: My Will is that Samuel's son William do get fifty pounds more than any one of the other children of my son Samuel and the remainder to be divided between William, Robert, Joseph, Margaret, Susanna, and Samuel or to their Legal Representatives share and share alike.

Item, I give and bequeath to my Daughter Esther Smith one full and equal sixth part of my Estate and my will is that my Daughter Esther nor her husband Robert Smith is not to receive any part of the principal of her share. I Nominate and appoint the Reverend Nathan Grier and Matthew Stanley trustees to take the care of the dividend of my Estate and it is to be put out at Interest by them and to be secured by Mortgage or in some other productive fund as [they] may think best and she the said Esther to get the income thereof as she stands in need at the discretion of the Trustees aforesaid and at her death to be equally divided among her children or their legal representatives share and share alike, But my Will is that if my daughter Esther should become a widow at any time during her life she is then to get the whole of the principal and interest that will then be in the hands of the Trustees aforesaid and at her disposal as she may think proper and her receipt shall be a full discharge to said Trustees.

Item I give and bequeath to my son Henry Kennedy and to his heirs and assigns one full equal sixth part of my Estate.

                    Appendix B

Will of William Kennedy, December 28, 1813, February 28, 1814, Will Book K-M, v 10-12 (1797-1817), Chester County, Pennsylvania, LDS Family History Library, Salt Lake City, Utah, Microfilm Roll 0020848.

Item I give and bequeath to my Daughter Susanna Kennedy and to her heirs and assigns five hundred dollars out of the [sale] of my Estate before any of the dividends is struck to any of my Children and also my will is that she get one full and equal sixth part of my Estate and my house clock, but she is not to get the clock until her mother's death without her consent. My will is that she get the above five hundred dollars for her services to me since she growed up over and above her sixth part.

Item I give and bequeath to my son William Kennedy clergyman and to his heirs and assigns one full equal sixth part of my Estate and lastly my will is that none of my children or grandchildren do get or receive any of their respective shares or legacies from my Executors until [they] have first given an obligation with approved security if Required to my wife their mother or grandmother as the case may be for the faithful payment of lawful interest to be paid to her annually on their Respective shares or legacies for her support and maintenance during her natural life and at her death to [cease] and be no more I nominate constitute and appoint my trusty friend Matthew Stanley of Brandywine township in the county and state aforesaid my whole and sole Executor of this my last will and Testament ratifying and confirming this and no other to be my last Will and Testament In Witness whereof I the said William Kennedy the Testator above named have here unto set my hand and seal this 28th day of December 1813.

William Kennedy (seal)

Signed sealed published pronounced by the said William Kennedy the Testator as and for his last Will and Testament in the presence of us - the interlining done before signing -James Long, William Willson, Alexander Long

West Chester February 28th 1814 Then personally appeared James Long, William Willson, Alexander Long who on their solemn oaths respectively did say that they were personally present and did see and hear William Kennedy the Testator in the foregoing Instrument of writing named sign seal publish pronounce and declare the same as and for his last Will and Testament and that at the doing thereof he was of sound and well disposing mind and memory to the best of their knowledge and belief.

Sworn [Cordm]
Charles Kenny Register

Be it remembered that on the 28th day of February Anno Domini 1814 The last Will and Testament of William Kennedy was proved in due form of Law and Letters Testamentary Thereon were duly granted to Matthew Stanley Esquire sole Executor therein named who was solemnly affirmed to exhibit a [true] and perfect inventory of the deceased estate into the Register's Office on or before the 28th day of March next and to settle the account of his Administration in one year from this time or when thereunto legally required Witness my hand and the seal of said office.

Charles Kenny Register

     Appendix B

January 11, 1974

TO WHOM IT MAY CONCERN:

This is to certify that one   W I L L M   K E N N E D Y   was enrolled as a Private, Second Class, Captain William Henry's First
Company, Eighth Battalion, Chester County Militia, according to
the evidence of a Return of the Classes of the Eighth Battalion
dated 1780.

HARRY E. WHIPKEY, Chief
Division of Archives & Manuscripts

<u>Authority</u>: Military Accounts
(<u>Militia</u>), Records of the Comptroller General, at the Division
of Archives & Manuscripts

<u>Residence ascribed:</u>
West Caln Township

Appendix C

Appendix C

Stephenie H. Tally-Frost, *Family Bible Records*, (Corpus Christi, Texas: Stephenie H. Tally-Frost, 1969), [DAR Library: GEN/VITAL/TAL], II:20.

The family record of Henry Kennedy & Elizabeth Wallace was found on old yellowed sheets of paper in the *Kennedy Family Bible*. There was no record of the publisher or date of publication in the Bible. The entries were copied by Jean B. Grube (Mrs. Joseph), 2834 Ruby Avenue, Fairbanks, Alaska 99701.

Grandfather William Kennedy d. 18 Feb 1814, age 78
Grandmother Susan Doak Kennedy d. 7 Dec 1821, age 79-1/2

(Other children unknown)
Henry, 28 Dec 1772, d. 11 Aug 1824, age 51 yr, 7 mo, 13 da.
Married 4 February 1796

(Both buried in Brandywine Churchyard, Chester Co., Pennsylvania)

[Grand]children:
William Wallace, 7 May 1797 - 15 Mar 1826
Robert, 28 May 1799 - 29 Nov 1804
Samuel Doak, 10 Apr 1801 - 13 Oct 1881 (80, 6, 3)
Mary, 27 Jun 1803 - 24 Jul 1804 (13 mo)
Mary W., 2 Jul 1805 - 16 Jul 1805 (15 da)
Robert Wallace, 2 Apr 1807 -
Elizabeth Wallace, 14 Aug 1809 -
Susan Doak, 1 Oct 1812 -
Mary Ann, 15 Jun 1815 - 23 Oct 1855 (40-3-8)
John, 23 Sep 1817 - 9 Nov 1884 (67-2-16)
Our seven mo. son was buried 30 Jul 1821
Jas. Henry, 16 Dec 1823 - 20 Mar 1824 (3 mo, 4-1/2 da)

Grandfather Robert Wallace d. 10 Feb 1799, age abt 77 yrs
Grandmother Mary Pickens Wallace d. 20 Aug 1814, age 83
Married 16 March 1749

Children:
Alexander, b. 15 May 1750, d. 13 Feb 1751
William, b. 11 Jan 1752
John, b. 16 Aug 1754
George, b. 27 Jun 1757
Elizabeth, b. 29 Apr 1760 (d. young)
Elizabeth, b. 24 Sep 1777, d. 14 Jan 1824, age 46 yr, 3 mo, 20 da

Note by Mrs. Grube: Elizabeth Wallace Kennedy m. Joseph Marvin Garvin. Their oldest son, George Samuel Garvin, b. 18 Feb 1856, m. Alvaretta "Allie" Gertrude Baumgardner in 1877. She was the oldest daughter of Daniel Harrison Baumgardner by his 1st wife. Mrs. Grube's husband, Joseph Grube, was the grandson of Daniel Harrison Baumgardner by his 2nd wife.

                              Appendix D

Appendix D

The silhouette of Peter Devlin was in the possession of the late Josephine Thompson Marshall, 121 Reillywood Avenue, Haddonfield, New Jersey, 08033-2201.

                                        Appendix E

Appendix E

QUAKER HERITAGE OF SUSAN (KENNEDY) DEVLIN

According to family legend, Susan (Kennedy) Devlin had Quaker as well as Scots-Irish Presbyterian connections.

The Family Legend - Conflicting Recollections

Four of the descendants of Susan (Kennedy) Devlin provided the following information about her alleged Quaker heritage:

William Scott Chambers recalled being told that Susan (Kennedy) Devlin was from a Quaker family. He further recalled being told that the Kennedy family owned a farm in Kennett Square, Chester County, Pennsylvania, where Peter Devlin was employed as a farm hand. Susan Kennedy was said to have run away with and married Peter Devlin over the objections of her parents who disinherited her. After Susan (Kennedy) Devlin's mother was widowed, his notes state that she married a man named "Allen from Blackwood."[1]

Josephine Thompson Marshall recalled that she was told by her maternal grandmother, Josephine Irene (Reitze) Chambers, that Susan (Kennedy) Devlin was from a Hicksite Quaker family. The family worshiped in a place called Newtown which she assumed to be in Bucks County. She said that her grandmother told her that Susan Kennedy met Peter Devlin at a school where he was employed as a gardener, but she does not know whether the school was in Newtown or somewhere in the City of Philadelphia.[2] She was told that Susan Kennedy ran away with and married Peter Devlin over the objections of her parents. After Susan (Kennedy) Devlin's mother, who was named Elizabeth, was widowed, she married a man named "Allen from Blackwood." She also recalled being told that Susan (Kennedy) Devlin's oldest child, a daughter named Lucy Devlin, was raised by her Quaker grandmother.[3]

David Harrington Marshall, Jr., recalled being told by his maternal great-grandmother, Josephine Irene (Reitze) Chambers, that Susan (Kennedy) Devlin's ancestors were Quakers who worshiped at Newton. He concluded that the

---

[1]Conversation on September 2, 1995, with the late William Scott Chambers, 9221 West Broward Boulevard, # 2510, Plantation, Florida 33324.

[2]Peter Devlin was not listed in the Philadelphia city directories as a gardener until 1855 some twenty years after he married Susan Kennedy.

[3]Conversation in March 1995, with the late Josephine Thompson Marshall, 121 Reillywood Avenue, Haddonfield, New Jersey 08033-2201.

reference was to the Newton Monthly Meeting in Haddonfield, New Jersey, and that Susan (Kennedy) Devlin's ancestors were likely Irish Quakers from Ulster.[4]

John J. Page recalled being told by his aunt, Catherine Irene (Reitze) Kelly, that his grandfather, John Francis Reitze had Quaker ancestors who arrived in the vicinity of Philadelphia sometime in the late-1600s "on the third Quaker ship." They may have been Germans who left Germany and went to Holland before coming to America. In fact, he was always under the impression that his grandfather, John Francis Reitze, was raised a Quaker. His grandfather was silent, very strict, and did not approve of drinking. He was also sent to live with family members in Lancaster at some point in his early life.[5]

FINDING THE QUAKER CONNECTION

The Possibilities

The following five possibilities were considered with respect to the Quaker connections of Susan (Kennedy) Devlin:

- Her father's maternal line.

- Her mother's side of the family which was probably Dutch or German.

- Her mother's second husband, "Allen from Blackwood."

- Her family's possible conversion to the Quaker faith after she was born.

- A collateral connection on her father's side of the family.

The Evidence

Given the abundance of Colonial, Revolutionary, and Quaker records covering southeastern Pennsylvania and South Jersey during the time period in question, it should have been possible to verify and document Susan (Kennedy) Devlin's Quaker heritage. In actual fact, however, the details concerning the Quaker connections of Susan (Kennedy) Devlin's family have stubbornly refused to yield to the investigative process and it has not been possible, to date, to trace the Quaker family connections with any certainty.

------

[4]Conversation on August 12, 1995, with David Harrington Marshall, Jr., 121 Reillywood Avenue, Haddonfield, New Jersey 08033-2201.

[5]Conversation on February 23, 1998, with John J. Page, 2524 Lombard Street, Philadelphia, Pennsylvania 19146-1025.

1. THE WELSH QUAKERS. The case for the Welsh Quakers in Chester County was considered in conjunction with the theory that Susan (Kennedy) Devlin's father's maternal ancestors may have been Quakers from Wales. This theory did not yield positive results.

Many of the Welsh emigrants to the vicinity of Chester County seem to have settled within the limits of the Welsh Tract, a barony or semi-independent government of 40,000 acres which William Penn set apart for the Welsh. An early description of these Welsh settlers in the Province of Pennsylvania is as follows:

> Among those early adventurers and settlers, who arrived about this time, were also many from Wales, of those who are called Ancient Britons, and mostly Quakers - Divers of those early Welsh settlers were persons of excellent and worthy character; and several of good education, family and estate. They had early purchased of the Proprietary, in England, forty thousand acres of land. Those who came at present took up so much of it in the West Side of the Sculkil *(sic)* River, as made the three townships of Merion, Haverford and Radnor, and a few years afterwards their number was so much augmented as to settle the three other townships of New-town *(sic)*, Goshen, and Uwchland. After this they continued still increasing, and became a numerous and flourishing people.[6]

According to Joseph Smith Harris, Susan (Kennedy) Devlin's great-great-grandparents were John and Emma (Parry) Vaughan.[7]

John Vaughan's family was Welsh Baptist. They came to America in search of religious freedom. They settled north of Downingtown in a hilly part of Chester County known as Uwchlan Township.

Emma Parry's family settled in Haverford Township where her father, Rowland Parry, was a tanner. The Parry family is believed to have been Welsh Presbyterian. Rowland Parry's will, dated February 10, 1714, begins with the words "In the Name of God Amen." This is an introductory phrase omitted in most Quaker wills. Emma Perry's brother, David Parry, was a captain in the Associate Regiments of Chester County during the Revolutionary War and her brother, John Parry, was buried in the Great Valley Presbyterian Church. Further, Emma Parry's brothers baptized their children in Christ Church and the First Presbyterian Church in Philadelphia.

---

[6]Thomas Allen Glenn, *Merion in the Welsh Tract with Sketches of the Townships of Haverford and Radnor - Historical and Genealogical Collections Concerning the Welsh Barony in the Province of Pennsylvania Settled by the Cymric Quakers in 1862*, (Norristown, Pennsylvania: Herald Press, 1896), 1.

[7]Joseph Smith Harris, *The Collateral Ancestry of Stephen Harris Born September 4, 1798 and of Marianne Smith Born April 2, 1805*, (Philadelphia, Pennsylvania: George F. Lasher, 1908), p. 67-71, 127-139.

John Vaughan appears to have married Emma Parry about 1728, but it was not until October 1756, six years after his death, that his widow and her daughter, Margaret Vaughan, became Baptists. They were admitted to the Great Valley Baptist Church in Chester County. On September 21, 1771, Emma (Parry) Vaughan transferred her membership to the Vincent Baptist Church which was nearer to her home. She remained a member of that church until her death in 1791.

2. THE DUTCH QUAKERS. The case for the Dutch Quakers was considered in conjunction with the theory that Susan (Kennedy) Devlin's mother, Elizabeth (Lambden) Kennedy may have had Dutch or German Quaker origins. This theory yielded two inconclusive results.

Dutch Quakers to Pennsylvania. The record indicates that after William Penn founded the province of Pennsylvania with English Quakers such as himself, he next turned his attention to attracting settlers from west Germany. The area had never recovered economically from the Thirty Years' War. Further, the religious settlement that followed the Peace of Westphalia in 1648 left thousands of devout Protestants belonging to small sects under the demands of established State churches which they found completely alien and unacceptable. William Penn's personal appearances in the Rhine country convinced many of the leaders of these people to come to America. Led by their ministers, great numbers began to arrive in 1683.[8]

The third Quaker ship to arrive on the Delaware River in 1683 was the Concord.[9] It departed Gravesend, England, on July 24, 1683, and arrived in Philadelphia on October 6th after a voyage of seventy-four days. Among its 140 passengers were thirty-three Dutch Quaker emigrants from Krefeld. This is consistent with family legend as related by John J. Page that the ancestors of Susan (Kennedy) Devlin were Quakers who arrived in the vicinity of Philadelphia sometime in the late-1600s "on the third Quaker ship."

Geographically, Krefeld is in the Rhineland. That is, Krefeld is about one-third of the way up the Rhine Valley from Rotterdam. Politically, the Krefelders were subjects of the Prince of Orange whose policy of toleration of Protestant sects resulted in a migration of people from Holland to Krefeld in the 17th Century.[10] Thus, in origin, language and customs, the Krefelders were Netherlanders and in religious affiliation they were Mennonite converts to the Quaker

---

[8]James G. Leyburn, *The Scots-Irish - A Social History*, (Chapel Hill, North Carolina: The University of North Carolina Press, 1962), 188.

[9]Marion Balderston, "Pennsylvania's 1683 Ships and Some of Their Passengers," *The Pennsylvania Genealogical Magazine*, 1965, 24 (2): 90.

[10]William I. Hull, *William Penn and the Dutch Quaker Migration to Pennsylvania*, (Swarthmore, Pennsylvania: 1935, reprint: Baltimore, Maryland: Genealogical Publishing Company, 1977), 189.

faith.[11]

On October 12, 1683, William Penn issued a land warrant for 6,000 acres in Germantown, one half of which was to go to the Krefelders and one half to be reserved for the Frankfort Company. The land was surveyed and measured off into fourteen plots. On October 25, 1683, the thirteen Krefeld pioneer men met with Francis Daniel Pastorius, a young German scholar and historian who was to become their spokesperson, at his home on the banks of the Delaware River to draw lots for the sites of their future homes.[12] The names of the thirteen Krefeld men were:

> Derick Isacks op den Graeff
> Herman Isacks op den Graeff
> Abraham Isacks op den Graeff
> Lenart Arents
> Thones Kunders
> Reiner Tijsen
> Willem Strepers
> Jan Lensen
> Pieter Keurlis
> Jan Siemes
> Johannes Blijkers
> Abraham Tunes
> Jan Luykens

Presently, the only surname from the list of pioneers that appears in connection with any of the descendants of Susan (Kennedy) Devlin is the surname Graeff which was used as the middle name of one of her great-grandsons, Henry Graef Chambers. If there is a connection between Susan (Kennedy) Devlin and the op den Graeff family, it should be noted that Derick and Herman appear to have left no descendants. Their brother, Abraham, broke with the Quakers about 1704 and died a Mennonite. He left three sons and a daughter named Margaret. His daughter married an Englishman named Thomas Howe who was a tailor in Germantown. The last that was heard from Abraham op den Graeff was in 1709 when he conveyed 300 acres of land to his daughter and her husband on condition that they take good care of him until his death.[13]

Dutch Quakers to Maryland. By 1662, Quaker and Presbyterian "dissenters" fleeing Episcopalian Virginia along with a few Huguenots were said to have been among the first settlers

---

[11]Hull, 179.

[12]Hull, 395.

[13]Hull, 218.

in Worcester County, Maryland.[14,15] It has been conjectured that Susan (Kennedy) Devlin's mother, Elizabeth (Lambden) Kennedy, may have descended from a family that lived in Worcester County during this time period.[16] Unfortunately, the ancestral lineage of Elizabeth (Lambden) Kennedy cannot be proven and no Quaker ancestors named Lambden (or Lampert), Dutch or otherwise, from Worcester County, Maryland, have been identified.

3. THE IRISH QUAKERS IN NEWTON, NEW JERSEY. The case for the Irish Quakers in Newton, New Jersey, was considered in conjunction with the theory that Susan (Kennedy) Devlin's Quaker connection may have been through her mother's second husband, "Allen from Blackwood."[17] This theory yielded inconclusive results.

Thomas Sharp of Dublin was one of the leaders of the Irish Quaker settlement in Newton, New Jersey. In 1718, he wrote the following account of the immigration and settlement in Newton of the five original Irish Quaker pioneer men and their families:

> Let it be remembered that upon the nineteenth day of September in the year of our Lord one thousand six hundred and eighty-one, **Mark Newby, William Bates, Thomas Thackara, George Goldsmith, and Thomas Sharp**, set saile from the Harbor belonging to the city of Dublin in the Kingdom of Ireland, in a pink called *The owner's adventure*, whereof Thomas Lurtin, of London, was commander, and being taken sick in the city, his mate John Dagger, officiated in his place; in order to transport us, and that we might settle ourselves in West Jersey, in America. And by the good providence of God we arrived in the Capes of Delaware the eighteenth day of November following, and so up the bay until we came to Elsenburg, and were landed with our goods and families at Salem, where we abode the winter. But it being very favourable weather and purchasing a boat amongst us, we had an opportunity to make a search up and down in that which was called the Third tenth, which had been reserved for the proprietors dwelling in Ireland, where we might find a place suitable for so many of us to settle down together, being in these early times somewhat doubtful of the Indians, and at last pitched down by that which is now called Newton creek, as the most invitingist place to settle down by, and then we went to Burlington, and

---

[14]Reginald V, Truitt and Millard G. Les Callette, *Worcester County, Maryland's Arcadia*. (Snow Hill, Maryland: Worcester County Historical Society, 1977), p unk.

[15]Worcester County, Maryland Genealogy, <<https://www.familysearch.org/wiki/en/Worcester_County,_Maryland_Genealogy>>, downloaded March 4, 2018.

[16]Kathryn Chambers Torpey, *William Kennedy of Chester County Pennsylvania, and His Descendants - A Compiled Genealogy (Including Davis, Smith, Wallace, Russell, and McClure),* (Alexandria, Virginia: Torpey Books, 2014), Chapter 4:195-196.

[17]Kathryn Chambers Torpey, *The Reitze Family in Philadelphia - Descended from Christopher Reitze Born 1824 in Hesse-Cassell, Germany,* (Alexandria, Virginia: Torpey Books, 2017), 13-16.

made application to the commissioners that we might have warrants directed to Daniel Leeds the Surveyor General, to survey unto every one of us, so much land as by the constitution at that time was allotted for a settlement being five hundred acres or that we had a right to, for a taking up it under, which accordingly we obtained.

At which time also Robert Zane, who came from the city of Dublin, and had been settled in Salem, four years before, joined in with us who had a right to a tenth, Mark Newby to a twentieth, William Bates to a twentieth, Thomas Thackara to a twentieth, Thomas Sharp (out of his uncle Anthony Sharp's right) a twentieth, and George Goldsmith (under the notion of Thomas Starkey's right) a tenth; all which of us excepting William Bates who took his on the southerly side of Newton creek, we took our land in one tract together for one thousand seven hundred and fifty acres, bounding in the forks of Newton creek and so over to Cooper's creek and by a line of marked trees to a small branch of the fork creek and so down the same as by the certificate of it standing upon record in the Secretary's office it doth appear. And after some time finding some inconveniency in having our land in common together being in the time settled at the place now called Newton in the manner of a town for fear as aforesaid at which being removed we come to an agreement to divide, George Goldsmith he chose the head of the creek. Thomas Sharp the forks or lower end of the land next towards the river by which means the rest kept to their settlements without any disadvantage to themselves.

And so the land was divided according to every man's right.[18]

This tiny settlement of Irish Friends, which is referred to in the records as being from Tipperary County in Ireland, joined the Newton Monthly Meeting.[19] In 1721, members of the Newton Monthly Meeting built a brick meeting house in Haddonfield on land donated by Elizabeth Haddon. From then forward, the Newton Monthly Meeting was held in Haddonfield. Gradually, the name Newton was dropped and the meeting became known as the Haddonfield Monthly Meeting.

A review was undertaken at Swarthmore College of the Orthodox and Hicksite records of the Haddonfield Monthly Meeting in an effort to determine whether Susan (Kennedy) Devlin's mother's second husband, "Allen from Blackwood" descended from any of these early Irish Quaker pioneers in Newton or whether the family of "Allen from Blackwood" may have

---

[18]Albert Cook Myers, *Immigration of the Irish to Pennsylvania 1682 - 1750 With Their Early History in Pennsylvania*, (Swarthmore, Pennsylvania: 1902, reprint: Baltimore, Maryland: Genealogical Publishing Company, 1969), 383.

[19]Michael J. O'Brien, *Irish Settlers in America - A Consolidation of Articles from the Journal of the American Irish Historical Society*, (Baltimore, Maryland: Genealogical Publishing Company, 1979), Volume II:93.

emigrated from Ireland to Newton at a later date.[20,21] Unfortunately, there was no mention of Elizabeth (Lambden) Kennedy's marriage to "Allen from Blackwood" in any of these records nor was there any mention of an Allen Collins or a Collins Allen that fit the profile of the man who married Elizabeth (Lambden) Kennedy.

4. THE IRISH QUAKERS IN KENNETT SQUARE, PENNSYLVANIA. The case for the Irish Quakers in Kennett Square was considered in conjunction with the theory that Susan (Kennedy) Devlin's family may have lived in Kennett Square and converted to the Quaker faith after she was born including the possibility that the conversion may have occurred after her mother was widowed. This theory did not yield positive results.

Chester County received a large part of the Irish Quaker migration. Early in the 18th Century, Quaker pioneers began moving in some substantial numbers from their old settlements in New Castle County, Delaware, and what is now known as Delaware County, Pennsylvania, to the wilds of Chester County. For some time, these Friends regularly made the difficult journey back to their old settlements to attend meetings. As more Quaker settlers arrived in the area of Chester County, the Friends began to hold meetings locally, in private homes. Later, these meetings were held in log houses and in buildings of brick and stone.[22]

The Newark Monthly Meeting (later known as the Kennett Monthly Meeting) was originally established in New Castle County, Delaware, in 1686. It included members from New Castle County and all of southern Chester County. It first met at the house of the widow Welsh in New Castle. At length it moved to Newark where it remained until 1707 when Vincent Caldwell, Thomas Wickersham, Joel Baily, Thomas Hope, Guyan Miller (an Irish Friend), and others living in Kennett Township and in the east end of Marlborough Township began holding meetings in private homes. In 1710, the Kennett Meeting House was built near Harmorton, in Chester County. Eventually the name Newark was dropped in favor of the name Kennett. One of the most eminent ministers of this meeting was Thomas Carleton, a native of King's County, Ireland.[23]

The index to the Kennett Monthly Meeting was examined for any evidence in support of

---

[20]Haddonfield Monthly Meeting: Minutes (Orthodox) 1827 to 1855; Births and Deaths (Orthodox) 1758 to 1803, Friends Historical Library of Swarthmore College, Swarthmore, Peensylvania 19081-1399.

[21]Haddonfield Monthly Meeting: Minutes (Hicksite) 1804 to 1813; 1814 to 1832; and 1832 to 1863, Friends Historical Library of Swarthmore College, Swarthmore, Pennsylvania 19081-1399.

[22]Myers, 125.

[23]Myers, 126.

                                                        Appendix F

the theory that Susan (Kennedy) Devlin's family belonged to the Kennett Monthly Meeting or lived anywhere near Kennett Square, a post-town of Kennett Township, about 30 miles southwest of Philadelphia.[24] There was no evidence that Susan (Kennedy) Devlin's parents lived in or near Kennett Square nor was there any evidence that her parents attended, converted or were members of the Kennett Monthly Meeting.[25] Further, there was no evidence that Susan (Kennedy) Devlin's mother may have converted to the Quaker faith after she was widowed.[26]

5. THE QUAKERS IN PHILADELPHIA. The case for the Quakers in Philadelphia was considered in conjunction with the theory that Susan (Kennedy) Devlin's Quaker connections may have been through collateral ancestors on her father's side of the family. This theory yielded positive results.

An examination of Quaker records in Philadelphia revealed that Susan (Kennedy) Devlin's first cousin, Samuel William Kennedy, the son of William Doak Kennedy and Ann Maria Sherborne, belonged to the Green Street Monthly Meeting in Philadelphia.

Samuel William Kennedy was married to Catharine Abercrombie Ridgway, the daughter of Richard Shreve Ridgway and Mary Ann Winkler. The couple was married on March 5, 1846 or March 15, 1846.[27,28] The Ridgways were Quakers from the Burlington Monthly Meeting in Burlington, New Jersey.

---

[24]Thomas F. Gordon, *A Gazetteer of the State of Pennsylvania*, (Philadelphia, Philadelphia: 1832, reprint: New Orleans, Louisiana: Polyanthos, Inc., 1975), 221.

[25]*The William Wade Hinshaw Index to Pennsylvania Quaker Meeting Records - Kennett Monthly Meeting Established 1686 as Newark Monthly Meeting (Name Changed 1760) in Chester County*, Volume IV: Removals 1751-1895; Marriages 1704-1937; Membership: Men's Minutes 1686-1897 and Women's Minutes 1699-1892. (Kokomo, Indiana: Selby Publishing and Printing, 1990).

[26]*The William Wade Hinshaw Index to Pennsylvania Quaker Meeting Records - Kennett Monthly Meeting Established 1686 as Newark Monthly Meeting (Name Changed 1760) in Chester County*, Volume IV: Removals 1751-1895; Marriages 1704-1937; Membership: Men's Minutes 1686-1897 and Women's Minutes 1699-1892. (Kokomo, Indiana: Selby Publishing and Printing, 1990).

[27]Joseph Smith Harris, *Record of the Smith Family Descended from John Smith Born 1655 in County Monaghan, Ireland*, (Philadelphia, Pennsylvania: Press of George F. Lasher, 1906), 83.

[28]Edna Letitia Kennedy Haydock, *The Kennedy Family*, (Haddonfield, New Jersey: Edna Haydock, Publisher, 1962), 12.

Samuel William Kennedy and Catharine Abercrombie Ridgway appear to have spent their entire married life in Philadelphia where they were members in good standing of the Green Street Monthly Meeting. In 1886, Samuel William Kennedy's obituary appeared in the *Friends' Intelligencer and Journal*. It read as follows:

> KENNEDY. - In Philadelphia, suddenly, Twelfth month 15th, Samuel W. Kennedy, aged 67; a member of the Monthly Meeting of Friends held at Green St.[29]

His widow's obituary appeared in the *Friends' Intelligencer*. It read as follows:

> KENNEDY. - Suddenly, Third month 22, 1899, at the residence of her son, Franklin W. Kennedy, Frankford, Philadelphia, Catharine A., widow of Samuel W. Kennedy, in her 72nd year; a valued member of the Monthly Meeting held at Green Street, Philadelphia.[30]

These are the only Quaker connections found thus far for Susan (Kennedy) Devlin.

---

[29]Obituary of Samuel William Kennedy, *Friends' Intelligencer and Journal*, Volume 43, 1886, p. 825, Swarthmore College, Friends Historical Library, Swarthmore, Pennsylvania 19081.

[30]Obituary of Catharine Abercrombie (Ridgway) Kennedy, *Friends' Intelligencer*, Volume 56, 1899, p. 248, Swarthmore College, Friends Historical Library, Swarthmore, Pennsylvania 19081.

BY: Kathryn C. Torpey,
         5035 Domain Place,
         Alexandria VA 22311

DATE: 10 April 2018

FOCUS: Susan (Kennedy) Devlin's relationship to the other persons buried in the same plot.

BACKGROUND: Susan (Kennedy) Devlin, the wife of Peter Devlin, died in Philadelphia on 4 April 1859. She was buried in Old Cathedral Cemetery in a plot owned by Ann Coleman (Section P, Range 5, Lot 21). There are eleven other persons buried in Old Cathedral Cemetery in the same plot with Susan (Kennedy) Devlin. Their relationship to Susan (Kennedy) Devlin is unknown.

METHODOLOGY: Research was conducted over a period of twenty years to determine the relationship of Susan (Kennedy) Devlin to the other persons buried in the plot. The Catholic Cemeteries Office was first contacted in 1995 and a plot profile was obtained. This was followed by an on-site visit to the cemetery where it was determined that no headstones or foot stones remain on the plot. In the early years, extensive research was conducted, onsite, at various facilities such as the Philadelphia City Archives, the Historical Society of Pennsylvania, the Genealogical Society of Pennsylvania and the Free Library of Philadelphia in an attempt to find published and unpublished records such as census enumerations, obituaries, death records, burial records, wills, probate records, city directories, naturalization records, marriage licenses, church records, etc., that might identify the relationship of Susan (Kennedy) Devlin to the other persons buried in the plot. Written requests were submitted to the Philadelphia Archdiocesan Historical Research Center for searches of their marriage and baptismal registers created prior to the year 1900 because those records were not open to the public at that time. This research methodology was repeated some years later using microfilm shipped from Salt Lake City to the McLean (Virginia) Family History Center and, again, prior to the publication of the Devlin family history, using online digitized sources, both indexed and unindexed.

RESEARCH RESULTS: The research yielded the following results concerning the persons listed in the plot profile provided by the Catholic Cemeteries Office on 5 October 1995.[1] The results are presented in the order the persons were buried in the plot beginning in 1853 and ending in 1966.

---

[1]Letter dated 5 October 1995 from the Catholic Cemeteries Office to Kathryn C. Hogan-Torpey containing a plot profile of Section P, Range 5, Lot 21 belonging to Ann Coleman (see Exhibit A).

NO.	NAME OF DECEASED	AGE	DATE OF BURIAL
1.	**COLEMAN, Mary**	**50 yrs**	**2 May 1853 (Should be 3 April 1853)**

Mary Coleman died on 1 April 1853 of a paoas abcess (sic).[2] The doctor's certificate accompanying the cemetery return states that Mary Coleman was a "Native" meaning she was born in the United States, about 1803. The place of Mary Coleman's death is indicated as Lloyd Street below Shippen. The address was in the Moyamensing District a very short distance from where Peter and Susan (Kennedy) Devlin lived until 1853. The only Mary Coleman found in the 1850 census schedule of the appropriate age living within the Moyamensing District (Ward 3) was stated to have been born in Ireland.[3] She appears to be enumerated with a daughter named Eliza Coleman.

Mary Coleman's obituary appeared in the *Philadelphia Public Ledger* on Saturday, 2 April 1853.[4] It read as follows:

> On the 1st inst., Mrs. Mary Coleman aged 50 years. The relatives and friends are respectfully invited to attend her funeral from the residence of Patrick Cassidy in Lloyd Street above Fitzwater, West of Broad, on Sunday afternoon at 1 o'clock without further notice. Funeral to proceed to Cathedral Cemetery.

NO.	NAME OF DECEASED	AGE	DATE OF BURIAL
2.	**COLEMAN, Catherine**	**23 yrs**	**20 November 1855**

According to the doctor's certificate that accompanied the cemetery return, Catherine Coleman died on 20 November 1855 of pneumonia.[5] The place of her death is indicated as the Philadelphia Hospital, Blockley.

---

[2]Philadelphia Cemetery Returns, Cathedral Cemetery Interments for the Week Ending 9 April 1853, Philadelphia City Archives, Philadelphia, Pennsylvania.

[3]1850 U.S. Census (population), Pennsylvania, Philadelphia County, Moyamensing, Ward 3, page 362B, lines 15-19, Household of Jackob Ermine, National Archives Microfilm Publication M432, Roll 809, contains the following reference:

> Mary Coleman   46 F   b. Ireland (sic)
> Eliza Coleman   14 F   b. Penn

[4]Obituary of Mary Coleman, *Philadelphia Public Ledger*, Saturday, 2 April 1853, Library of Congress, Newspaper Reading Room, Washington, D.C.

[5]Philadelphia Cemetery Returns, Cathedral Cemetery Interments for the Week Ending 24 November 1855, Philadelphia City Archives, Philadelphia Pennsylvania.

                                    Appendix G

The 1850 census schedule shows that she was an 18 year old servant living in Moyamensing District (Ward 4) in the home of Patrick Cassidy, County Prison K[eeper].[6] The census indicates she was born in Pennsylvania about 1832.

3.　　**DEVLIN, Susan**　　　　**44 yrs**　　　**1 May 1859 (Should be 5 April 1859)**

Susan (Kennedy) Devlin was born circa 1815 in Pennsylvania and died on April 4, 1859 in Philadelphia, Pennsylvania. She marred Peter Devlin on 19 May 1835 in Philadelphia, Pennsylvania. He was born circa 1810 in Ireland and may have died on 3 January 1864 probably in Philadelphia, Pennsylvania. She was buried in this plot in Old Cathedral Cemetery. The burial place of her husband, Peter Devlin, is unknown. The details of her life are contained in the following two **authored narratives**: *William Kennedy of Chester County, Pennsylvania, and His Decendants - A Compiled Genealogy (Including Davis, Smith, Wallace, Russell, and McClure)* and *The Devlin Family in Philadelphia Descended from Peter Devlin Born c 1810 in Ireland* [7,8]

4.　　**DEVLIN, James**　　　　**70 yrs**　　　**27 March 1871**

The Old Cathedral Cemetery burial register states this James Devlin was a 70 year old male who was buried on Monday, 27 (sic) March 1871 in Section P, Range 5, Lot 21.[9,10] The physician's certificate confirms that he was a 70 year old male. It further states that he died at 1631 N. 15th Street (Ward 20) of unknown causes

---

[6]1850 U.S. Census (population), Pennsylvania, Philadelphia County, Moyamensing, Ward 4, page 443A, lines 36-42, Household of Patrick Cassiday, National Archives Microfilm Publication M432, Roll 809.

[7]Kathryn C. Torpey, *William Kennedy of Chester County, Pennsylvania, and His Decendants - A Compiled Genealogy (Including Davis, Smith, Wallace, Russell, and McClure),* (Alexandria, Virginia: Torpey Books, 2014), p. 203-216.

[8]Kathryn C. Torpey, *The Devlin Family in Philadelphia Descended from Peter Devlin Born c 1810 in Ireland,* (Alexandria, Virginia: Torpey Books, 2018), p. 32-53.

[9]Old Cathedral Cemetery Burial Register, image 4746, Pennsylvania and New Jersey, Church and Town Records, 1669-2013, <<www.ancestry.com>, downloaded 26 February 2018.

[10]Old Cathedral Cemetery Alphabetical Index to Burials, Reel 835, image 1153, Pennsylvania and New Jersey, Church and Town Records, 1669-2013, <<www.ancestry.com>, downloaded 26 February 2018, erroneously states the burial of James Devlin occurred on 27 March 1870 (sic).

and was buried Sunday, 26 (sic) March 1871.[11]

No obituary for this James Devlin appeared in the *Philadelphia Public Ledger* or the *Philadelphia Inquirer* on Friday, 24 March 1871, Saturday, 25 March 1871, or Monday, 27 March 1871.

An 1871 estate file exists in the City and County of Philadelphia for a James Devlin, but it is dated 12 January 1871 which is over two months before this James Devlin was buried in Old Cathedral Cemetery.[12]

The 1870 U.S. census schedule contains one possibility for this James Devlin that is inconclusive.[13]

5.   DEVLIN, James   72 yrs   24 April 1872

Adding to the mystery, the Catholic Cemeteries Office reports that this James Devlin was a 72 year old male who was buried in the following two cemeteries on the same date:

- Old Cathedral Cemetery (Section P, Range 5, Lot 21)[14,15]

---

[11]Philadelphia Cemetery Returns, Cathedral Cemetery Interments for the Week Ending 1 April 1871, Philadelphia City Archives, Philadelphia, Pennsylvania, Microfilm Roll 2020824.

[12]Estate of James Devlin, # 25, 12 January 1871, Admin T-479, Register of Wills for the City and County of Philadelphia, Philadelphia, Pennsylvania, states that a Francis J. Devlin of Kings County, New York, the only child and heir of James Devlin, deceased, renounced his rights to Letters of Administration upon the estate of his father in favor of Edward A. Muldoon of the City and County of Philadelphia.

[13]1870 U. S. Census (population), First Enumeration, Pennsylvania, Philadelphia County, City of Philadelphia, Ward 20, page 585B, line 24, House of the Poor, National Archives Microfilm Publication M593, Roll 1407, says:

James DEVLIN   71 W M   b. Ireland   House of the Poor

[14]Old Cathedral Cemetery Alphabetical Index to Burials, Reel 835, image 4844, line 7 [right side], Pennsylvania and New Jersey, Church and Town Records, 1669-2013, <<www.ancestry.com>, downloaded 26 February 2018.

[15]Old Cathedral Cemetery Burial Register, image 4794, line 17, Pennsylvania and New Jersey, Church and Town Records, 1669-2013, <<www.ancestry.com>>, downloaded 26 February 2018. NOTE: the entry is erroneously indexed by ancestry.com as 24 JAN 1872.

- New Cathedral Cemetery (Section H, Range 6, Lot 19).[16,17]

No connection has been found between the two cemetery plots except that one of Susan (Kennedy) Devlin's grandsons (i.e., Charles Reitze), was buried in the plot at New Cathedral Cemetery.[18]

Unfortunately, the name of this John Devlin does not appear in the Philadelphia death index. There is no record of his death in the cemetery returns for either Old Cathedral Cemetery or New Cathedral Cemetery for the week ending 27 April 1872.[19,20] And, no obituary for him appeared in the *Philadelphia Public Ledger* or the *Philadelphia Inquirer*.

The 1870 U.S. census schedule is inconclusive with respect to this James Devlin.[21]

---

[16]New Cathedral Cemetery Alphabetical Index to Burials, line 15 [right side], Reel 836, image 55, Pennsylvania and New Jersey, Church and Town Records, 1669-2013, <<www.ancestry.com>, downloaded 26 February 2018.

[17]New Cathedral Cemetery Burial Register, image 1954, line 3 (right side], Pennsylvania and New Jersey, Church and Town Records, 1669-2013, <<www.ancestry.com>>, downloaded 26 February 2018.

[18]Kathryn Chambers Torpey, *The Reitze Family in Philadelphia - Descended from Christopher Reitze Born 1824 in Hesse-Cassell, Germany*, (Alexandria, Virginia: Torpey Books, 2017), 42-43 contains a profile of the plot at New Cathedral Cemetery (Section H, Range 6, Lot 19) belonging to Ellen Creedon where this unknown James Devlin is buried along with seven others including Charles Reitz (sic), son of Lucy (Devlin) Reitze and grandson of Susan (Kennedy) Devlin.

[19]Philadelphia Cemetery Returns, Cathedral Cemetery Interments for the Week Ending April 27, 1872, Philadelphia City Archives, Philadelphia, Pennsylvania, FHL Microfilm Roll 2021140, digital image 199-200, <<www.familysearch.org>>, downloaded February 26, 2018.

[20]Philadelphia Cemetery Returns, New Cathedral Cemetery Interments for the Week Ending April 27, 1872, Philadelphia City Archives, Philadelphia, Pennsylvania, FHL Microfilm Roll 2021140, digital image 494, <<www.familysearch.org>>, downloaded February 26, 2018.

[21]1870 U. S. Census (population), First Enumeration, Pennsylvania, Philadelphia County, City of Philadelphia, Ward 20, page 585B, line 24, House of the Poor, National Archives Microfilm Publication M593, Roll 1407, says:

James DEVLIN   71 W M   b. Ireland   House of the Poor

          Appendix G

6.   **COLEMAN, Anna**   **60 yrs**   **3 March 1892**

Anna Coleman died on 29 February 1892 from chronic disease of the kidneys. She was stated to be a 60 year old widow born in England (sic). She was living at 2001 Pine Street at the time of her death.[22,23] She was buried on 3 March 1892.[24] There was no obituary published in the *Philadelphia Inquirer* or *The Times* to commemorate her passing.

In the 1860 census, she was enumerated as Ann *Coleman*.[25] In the 1870 census (First and Second Enumerations), she was enumerated as Anna *Coleman*.[26,27] In the 1880 census, she was enumerated as Anna *Albach*, widow.[28]

There is a discrepancy between the 1870 and the 1880 census with respect to where her parents were born. The 1870 census (First Enumeration) does *not* indicate her parents were foreign born whereas the 1880 census states they were born in Ireland.

---

[22]Philadelphia Cemetery Returns, Cathedral Cemetery Interments for the Week Ending March 5, 1872, Philadelphia City Archives, Philadelphia, Pennsylvania, FHL Microfilm Roll 1889223, digital image 353, <<www.familysearch.org>>, downloaded February 27, 2018.

[23]Philadelphia Death Register, Philadelphia City Archives, Philadelphia, Pennsylvania, FHL Microfilm Roll 1011818, digital image 190, <<www.familysearch.org>>, downloaded February 26, 2018.

[24]Old Cathedral Cemetery Burial Register, image 1411, line 16, Pennsylvania and New Jersey, Church and Town Records, 1669-2013, <<www.ancestry.com>, downloaded February 27, 2018.

[25]1860 U.S. Census (population), Pennsylvania, Philadelphia County, City of Philadelphia, Ward 8, page 609, lines 35-37, Household of Ann Coleman, National Archives Microfilm Publication M653, Roll 1158.

[26]1870 U.S. Census (population), First Enumeration, Pennsylvania, Philadelphia County, City of Philadelphia, Ward 8, page 192B, lines 23-25, Household of Eugene Franssen, National Archives Microfilm Publication M593, Roll 1393.

[27]1870 U.S. Census (population), Second Enumeration, Pennsylvania, Philadelphia County, City of Philadelphia, Ward 8, page 7A, lines 17-21, Household of Eugene Franssen, National Archives Microfilm Publication M593, Roll 1421.

[28]1880 U.S. Census (population), Pennsylvania, Philadelphia County, City of Philadelphia, Ward 8, page 450C, lines 11-15, Household of Eugene Franssen, National Archives Microfilm Publication T9, Roll 1171.

7.   FRANSSEN, Eugene   80 yrs   14 July 1898

Eugene Franssen was the husband of Elizabeth (Coleman) Franssen and the father of Anna Pauline (Franssen) Coll. They are all buried in this plot.

The *Genealogy of the Franssen Family of Telegen, Limburg, The Netherlands* contains the following information about Eugene Franssen:

> Eligius Petrus Henricus Franssen, b. June 30, 1819, Goch; d. July 12, 1907 (sic), Philadelphia, Pennsylvania; he moved from Xanten to America in 1851 to avoid conscription and settled in Philadelphia; m (1) Josephina Carters (sic), February 1, 1853, who died a few months later of brain fever; m (2) Elisabeth Coleman, 1859 (sic); b. February 26, 1836, Philadelphia, Pennsylvania; d. September 9, 1897 (sic), Philadelphia, Pennsylvania.[29]

The first wife of Eugene Franssen was Anna Josephine Carter. She was the daughter of Bernard Moore Carter and Lucy Grymes Lee; the granddaughter of General "Lighthorse" Harry Lee; and the niece of General Robert E. Lee.[30] Anna Josephine (Carter) Franssen died on 2 April 1853 in Philadelphia.[31] She was buried in a plot (Lot 61, Section B) belonging to her brother, Charles H. Carter, at Laurel Hill Cemetery alongside her mother and father and her sister, Madame Mildred Randolph (Carter) De Potestad.[32] The cause of death was listed as disease of the brain.[33] She was 41 years old. Eugene and Anna Josephine (Carter)

---

[29]M. Hub. M. Michels, *Genealogie der Familie Franssen te Tegelen van 1651 tot heden [Genealogy of the Franssen Family of Telegen, Limburg, The Netherlands]*, (n.p.: n.p., 1914), p. 56-57, FHL Microfilm Roll 1183612.

[30]Florence Tyler Carlton, compiler, *A Genealogy of the Known Descendents of Robert Carter of Corotoman*, (Irvington, Virginia: Foundation for Historic Christ Church, Inc., 1982), p. 55.

[31]Obituary of Anna Josephine Franssen, *Philadelphia Public Ledger*, Thursday, April 7, 1853 p. 2, Library of Congress, Newspaper Reading Room, Washington, D.C., says:

> On Saturday afternoon the 2nd inst., Anna Josephine Carter, wife of Eugene Franssen of Prussia.

[32]Letter received December 16, 1999, from Laurel Hill Cemetery, 3822 Ridge Avenue, Philadelphia, Pennsylvania 19132-1881 concerning burials in North Laurel Hill Cemetery, Lot 61, Section B belonging to Charles H. Carter.

[33]Philadelphia Cemetery Returns, Laurel Hill Cemetery Interments for the Week Ending April 9, 1853, Philadelphia City Archives, Philadelphia, Pennsylvania.

Franssen had no children.

The date Eugene Franssen married his second wife, Elizabeth Coleman, is not known, but he appears to have been living adjacent to her and his future sister-in-law, Anna Coleman, and her daughter, Elizabeth Coleman, as early as 1860.[34] Thereafter, they are always enumerated living together.[35,36,37] They were even listed together in the 1885 Philadelphia Blue Book. It read as follows:

> 1506 Locust Street
> Mr. & Mrs. Eugene Franssen
> Ms. Annie Coleman[38]

Eugene Franssen was a Prussian count.[39] He submitted his Declaration of Intent on 30 March 1853 just before the death of his first wife. He was naturalized on 27 April 1860 at the Supreme Court of Pennsylvania thus relinquishing his allegiance to the King of Prussia and his title.[40]

---

[34]1860 U.S. Census (population), Pennsylvania, Philadelphia County, City of Philadelphia, Ward 8, page 609, lines 35-37, Household of Wm. Dougherty, National Archives Microfilm Publication M653, Roll 1158.

[35]1870 U.S. Census (population), First Enumeration, Pennsylvania, Philadelphia County, City of Philadelphia, Ward 8, page 192B, lines 23-25, Household of Eugene Franssen, National Archives Microfilm Publication M593, Roll 1393.

[36]1870 U.S. Census (population), Second Enumeration, Pennsylvania, Philadelphia County, City of Philadelphia, Ward 8, page 7A, lines 17-21, Household of Eugene Franssen, National Archives Microfilm Publication M593, Roll 1421.

[37]1880 U.S. Census (population), Pennsylvania, Philadelphia County, City of Philadelphia, Ward 8, page 450C, lines 11-15, Household of Eugene Franssen, National Archives Microfilm Publication T9, Roll 1171.

[38]*Boyd's Blue Book: The Fashionable Private Address Directory and Ladies' Visiting and Shopping Guide of Philadelphia and Surroundings. The Names of 20,000 Prominent Householders, Arranged Alphabetically and Classified by Streets*, (Philadelphia, Pennsylvania: C.E. Howe Company, 1885).

[39]Florence Tyler Carlton, compiler, *A Genealogy of the Known Descendents of Robert Carter of Corotoman*, (Irvington, Virginia: Foundation for Historic Christ Church, Inc., 1982), p. 60.

[40]P. William Filby, *Philadelphia Naturalization Records: An Index to Records of Aliens Declarations of Intention and/or Oaths of Allegiance, 1780-1880*, (Detroit, Michigan: Gale

Eugene Franssen founded the Teutonia Fire Insurance Company where he served as president until his death on 11 July 1898.[41,42] The following announcement was published by the company in *The Times* to commemorate his passing:

OFFICE OF THE TEUTONIA FIRE INSURANCE CO., 424 WALNUT ST.
Philadelphia, July 15, 1898

At a special meeting of the Board of Directors of the TEUTONIA FIRE
INSURANCE COMPANY, held this day, the following resolutions were passed
and spread upon the minutes:

WHEREAS, It having pleased Devine Providence to take from us Mr. EUGENE
FRANSSEN, our honored President, therefore be it

RESOLVED, That we the officers and members of the Board of Directors
hereby express our deep sorrow at the loss sustained by the company, family,
friends, and the community.

During a period of 27 years Mr. FRANSSEN devoted himself to the interests of
the company. His integrity of purpose, punctilious sense of honor, unobtrusive
charity and love of truth commanded the respect of all who knew him and be it
further

RESOLVED, That these resolutions be engrossed and tendered the bereaved
family as a mark of our deep sympathy.

C. WILLIAM BERGNER, Vice President
Attest: THOMAS CHAMBERLAIN, Secretary[43]

The obituary of Eugene Franssen appeared in the *Philadelphia Inquirer* on Wednesday, 13 July 1898. It read as follows:

FRANSSEN - On July 11, 1898, Eugene Franssen. The
relatives and friends are invited to attend the funeral
Thursday morning at 8:30 o'clock from his late residence at
2001 Pine Street. Services at St. Patrick's Church at 10

Research Company, 1982), p. 201.

[41]Scharf and Westcott, *History of Philadelphia: 1609-1884*, 3 volumes (Philadelphia, Pennsylvania: Everts and Company, 1884), p. 2126.

[42]1898 Death Index, City of Philadelphia, page 1269, 16 July 1898, Philadelphia City Archives, Philadelphia, Pennsylvania.

[43]Announcement, *The Times*, Philadelphia, Pennsylvania, Saturday, 16 July 1898, p. 9, <<www.newspaperarchive.com>>, downloaded 7 March 2018.

o'clock. Interment private.[44]

Eugene Franssen died intestate. His daughter, Anna Pauline Franssen, filed an application for letters of administration on 18 July 1898, to settle his estate.[45] His widow, Elizabeth Franssen, renounced her right to letters of administration in favor of her daughter on the same date. The Teutonia Fire Insurance Company of which Eugene Franssen had been president since its incorporation on 7 August 1871 was granted permission to dissolve by the Commons Pleas Court of Philadelphia on 15 February 1902.[46]

8.   FRANSSEN, Elizabeth   59 yrs   13 September 1898

According to the 1850, 1860, 1870, and 1880 census schedules cited earlier, Elizabeth (Coleman) Franssen was born in Pennsylvania. There is, however, a discrepancy between the 1870 and 1880 census schedules with respect to where her parents were born. For more information about the discrepancy, see item 6.

Elizabeth Franssen died, suddenly, in Atlantic City, on 9 September 1898 two months after the death of her husband.[47] Her obituary appeared in *The Times* on 12 September 1898. It read as follows:

> FRANSSEN - On September 9, 1898, suddenly, at Atlantic City,
> N.J., ELIZABETH, widow of Eugene Franssen. The relatives
> and friends are invited to attend the funeral, on Thursday morning
> at 8:30 o'clock from her residence, 2001 Pine street. Services at
> St. Patrick's Church at 10 A.M. Interment private.[48]

---

[44]Obituary of Eugene Franssen, *Philadelphia Inquirer*, Wednesday, 13 July 1898, p. 10, Library of Congress, Newspaper Reading Room, Washington, D.C.

[45]Estate of Eugene Franssen, No. 815, 1898 (Admin Book 5-525; Inv Book 28-540), Register of Wills Archives, Philadelphia, Philadelphia County, Pennsylvania

[46]News Story, *The Times*, Philadelphia, Pennsylvania, Saturday, 15 February 1902, p. 1, <<www.newspapers.com>>, downloaded 1 March 2018.

[47]Death of Elizabeth Franssen, 9 September 1898, Atlantic City, Atlantic County, New Jersey, Division of Archives and Record Management, New Jersey Department of State, Trenton, New Jersey, FHL Microfilm Roll 589810, digital image 29, <<www.familysearch.org>>, downloaded 2 March 2018.

[48]Obituary of Elizabeth Franssen, *The Times*, Philadelphia, Pennsylvania, Monday, 12 September 1898, p. 8, <<www.newspapers.com>>, downloaded 2 March 2018.

9.   COLL, Anna   59 yrs   23 February 1925

Anna Coll was the daughter of Eugene Franssen and Elizabeth (Coleman) Franssen.[49] Her birth name was Anna Pauline Franssen. She married James Frederick Coll, a dentist, on 12 July 1902.[50] They had three children, James F. Coll, Jr., born 19 May 1903, and Francis B. Coll, and Anne P. Coll, twins, born 24 (sic) March 1906.[51] She died on 19 February 1825. Her obituary appeared in the *Philadelphia Inquirer* on Saturday, 21 February 1925. It read as follows:

> COLL - Feb. 19, ANNA PAULINE FRANSSEN, wife of Dr.
> James Frederick Coll. Relatives and friends are invited to
> attend the funeral, Mon. 8:30 A.M. from her late residence,
> 2001 Pine St. Mass of Solemn Requiem at St. Patrick's
> Church, 10 A.M. Int. Cathedral Cemetery.[52]

10.   COLL, James   25 days   8 October 1931

James Coll was the grandson of Anna Pauline (Franssen) Coll and the son of James F. Coll, Jr, and his wife, Evelyn A. Merritt. He was born prematurely on 13 September 1931 and died on 6 October 1931.[53]

----

[49]1880 U.S. Census (population), Pennsylvania, Philadelphia County, City of Philadelphia, Ward 8, page 450C, lines 11-15, Household of Eugene Franssen, National Archives Microfilm Publication T9, Roll 1171.

[50]1902 Marriage License Applications, City of Philadelphia, License No. 148292, Philadelphia City Archives, Philadelphia, Pennsylvania.

[51]M. Hub. M. Michels, *Genealogie der Familie Franssen te Tegelen van 1651 tot heden [Genealogy of the Franssen Family of Telegen, Limburg, The Netherlands]*, (n.p.: n.p., 1914), p. 56-57, FHL Microfilm Roll 1183612.

[52]Obituary of Anna Pauline Franssen Coll, *Philadelphia Inquirer*, Saturday, 21 February 1925, p. 26 and Sunday, 22 February 1925, p. 18, Library of Congress, Newspaper Reading Room, Washington, D.C.

[53]Pennsylvania, Death Certificates, 1906-1964, Pennsylvania Historic and Museum Commission, Harrisburg, Pennsylvania, re: James Frederick Coll, 3rd, 6 October 1931, Philadelphia, Philadelphia County, Pennsylvania.

11.   COLEMAN, Elizabeth   75 yrs (sic)   10 December 1946

Elizabeth Coleman died 5 December 1946.[54] Her obituary appeared in the
Philadelphia Inquirer on Sunday, 8 December 1946. It read as follows:

> Coleman - Dec. 5 at her home 2050 Rittenhouse Square, Miss
> Elizabeth Coleman. Funeral Tuesday morning William V Lynch's
> Sons, 270 S. 20th St. Mass of Solemn Requiem Church of St. Patrick
> 10 A.M. Interment Cathedral Cemetery. Friends may call Mon 7-9
> P.M.[55]

Her death certificates states she was 75 at the time of her death. Based on an
examination of the following censuses, she was probably closer to 90 years old:

> 1860: 4 years old (b. 1856)[56]
> 1870: 14 years old (b. 1856)[57]
> 1880: 20 years old (b. 1860) - enumerated as Elizabeth *Albach*[58]
> 1900: 39 years old (b. 1860)[59]

---

[54]Death Certificate for Elizabeth Coleman, 5 December 1946, # 109454 & 23441,
Pennsylvania Vital Statistics, New Castle, Pennsylvania 16103 says birth date *unknown* and
parents' names *unknown*. The informant, Ann (sic) Coll, is also buried in this plot.

[55]Obituary of Elizabeth Coleman, *Philadelphia Inquirer*, Sunday, 8 December 1946, p. S-
9 and Monday, 9 December 1946, p. 13, Library of Congress, Newspaper Reading Room,
Washington, D.C.

[56]1860 U.S. Census (population), Pennsylvania, Philadelphia County, City of
Philadelphia, Ward 8, page 609, lines 35-37, Household of Ann Coleman, National Archives
Microfilm Publication M653, Roll 1158.

[57]1870 U.S. Census (population), Second Enumeration, Pennsylvania, Philadelphia
County, City of Philadelphia, Ward 8, page 7A, lines 17-21, Household of Eugene Franssen,
National Archives Microfilm Publication M593, Roll 1421.

[58]1880 U.S. Census (population), Pennsylvania, Philadelphia County, City of
Philadelphia, Ward 8, page 450C, lines 11-15, Household of Eugene Franssen, National Archives
Microfilm Publication T9, Roll 1171.

[59]1900 U.S. Census (population), Pennsylvania, Philadelphia County, City of
Philadelphia, Ward 7, E.D. 136, page 3, lines 98-100, Household of Anna P. T. Franssen,
National Archives Microfilm Publication T623, Roll 1455.

Anna P T. Franssen	32y	Sep 1867 head	PA GER PA
Elizabeth Coleman	39y	July 1860 cousin	PA GER PA
Catherine Kane	40y	Dec 1859 servant	PA IRE IRE

1910: 26 years old (b. 1884)[60]
1920: 59 years old (b. 1861)[61]
1930: 73 years old (b. 1857)[62]
1940: 83 years old (b. 1857)[63] - enumerated with Anna (sic) P. Coll, niece (sic)

12.   COLL, Anne P.   59 yrs   14 May 1966

Anne P. Coll was the daughter of Anna Pauline (Franssen) Coll. She was first enumerated in the 1910 census with her parents, both her brothers, and her cousin, Elizabeth Coleman. She never married. She may have been living with her father, James F. Coll, at 2050 Rittenhouse Square at the time of his death on 7 March 1959.[64]

She died on 11 May 1966. Her obituary appeared in the *Philadelphia Inquirer* on Saturday, 14 May 1966. It read as follows:

> COLL. On May 11, 1966, ANNE P., daughter of the late Dr. James F. and Ann Coll (nee Fransen) (sic). Relatives and friends are invited to attend the funeral Sat. 8:30 A.M. from William H. Logan, 2410 Lombard St. Solemn High Mass of Requiem, St. Patrick's Church, 10 A.M. Int. Old Cathedral Cem. Friends may call Friday evening.[65]

---

[60]1910 U.S. Census (population), Pennsylvania, Philadelphia County, City of Philadelphia, Ward 7, E.D. 108, page 4B, lines 94-99, Household of James F. Coll, National Archives Microfilm Publication T624, Roll 1388.

[61]1920 U.S. Census (population), Pennsylvania, Philadelphia County, City of Philadelphia, Ward 7, E.D. 165, page 3B, lines 79-84, Household of James F. Coll, National Archives Microfilm Publication T625, Roll 1618.

[62]1930 U.S. Census (population), Pennsylvania, Philadelphia County, City of Philadelphia, Ward 7, E.D. 281, page 4B, lines 82-86, Household of James F. Coll, National Archives Microfilm Publication T626, Roll 1618.

[63]1940 U.S. Census (population), Pennsylvania, Philadelphia County, City of Philadelphia, Ward 8, E.D. 51-159, page 1A, lines 3-4, Household of Elizabeth Coleman, National Archives Microfilm Publication T627, Roll 3692.

[64]Obituary of Dr. James Frederick Coll, *Philadelphia Inquirer*, Monday, 9 March 1959, <<www.newspapers.com>>, downloaded 9 April 2018

[65]Obituary of Anne P. Coll, *Philadelphia Inquirer*, Saturday, 14 May 1966, p. 10, Library of Congress, Newspaper Reading Room, Washington, D.C.

DISCUSSION

A hypothetical descendant chart was created based on the results of the research (see Exhibit B). The primary person of interest was Mary Coleman and her relationship to the other persons buried in the plot. **It was hypothesized that Mary Coleman might be the mother of Catherine Coleman, Anna Coleman, and Elizabeth (Coleman) Franssen and the sister of Peter Devlin.**

The research revealed that Mary Coleman was enumerated in the 1850 census with a youngster named Eliza Coleman, aged 14 b. PA, and that Mary Coleman was buried in 1853 from the residence of Patrick Cassidy, the county prison keeper, with whom a young woman named Catherine Coleman, aged 18 b. PA, was enumerated in the 1850 census. **This evidence suggests, but does not prove, that Mary Coleman might have been the mother of both these two young women and that they might be buried in this plot under the names Elizabeth (Coleman) Franssen and Catherine Coleman.**

The identify of Anna Coleman and her relationship to Mary Coleman is more complex. Anna Coleman may have owned the plot in Old Cathedral Cemetery where everyone is buried. Furthermore, Anna Coleman and Elizabeth (Coleman) Franssen appear to have lived together from 1860 until their death. **This evidence suggests, but does not prove, that Anna Coleman could have been the daughter of Mary Coleman and the sister of Elizabeth (Coleman) Franssen and Catherine Coleman.**

Regardless of how Mary Coleman may be related to Elizabeth (Franssen) Coleman, Catherine Coleman, and Anna Coleman, there is no evidence that these women are related to Susan (Kennedy) Devlin or her husband, Peter Devlin.

The identity of the two James Devlins buried in this plot could not be determined. There is no evidence that they are related to Susan (Kennedy) Devlin or her husband, Peter Devlin.

The identify and relationship of the remaining persons buried in this plot are understood, but do not yield any evidence that they are related to Susan (Kennedy) Devlin or her husband, Peter Devlin.

CONCLUSION

The relationship of Susan (Kennedy) Devlin to any of the individuals buried in this plot remains unknown.

Appendix G

Burials in Old Cathedral Cemetery in the
Plot Belonging to Ann Coleman
(Section P, Range 5, Lot 21)

EXHIBIT A

SUBJECT:

Sec. P, Range 5, Lot 21

Lot Holder- Ann Coleman

TO:

FROM: Cathedral Cemetery

NAME	AGE	DATE OF INTERMENT	GRAVE
Franssen Eugene	80 Yrs.	7-14-1898	East
Franssen Elizabeth	59 Yrs.	9-13-1898	"
Coll Anne P.	59 Yrs.	5-14-1966	"
Coleman Catherine	23 Yrs.	11-20-1855	2-East
Coll Anna	59 Yrs.	2-23-1925	"
Coll James	25 Days	10-8-1931	"
Devlin James	70 Yrs.	3-27-1871	2-West
Devlin James	72 Yrs.	4-24-1872	"
Coleman Anna	60 Yrs.	3-3-1892	"
Devlin Susan	44 Yrs.	5-1-1859	West
Coleman Elizabeth	75 Yrs.	12-10-1946	"
Coleman Mary	50 Yrs.	5-2-1853	"

Appendix G

EXHIBIT B

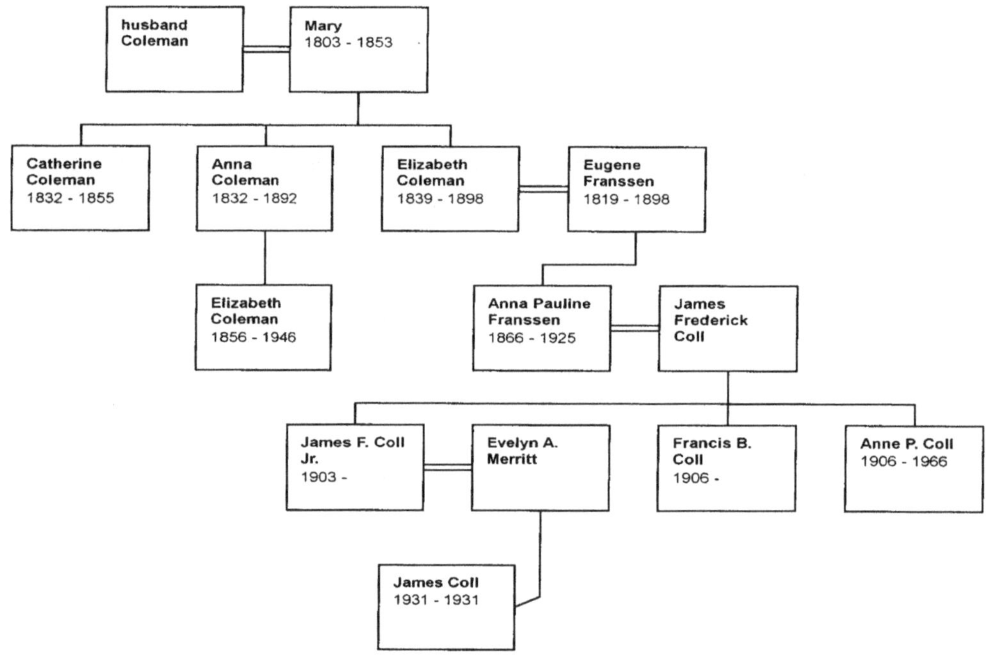

Appendix G

Descendants of Susan (Kennedy) Devlin

Generation 1

1. **SUSAN[1] KENNEDY** was born about 1815 in Pennsylvania. She died on 04 Apr 1859 in Philadelphia, Pennsylvania. She married Peter Devlin on 19 May 1835 in Philadelphia, Pennsylvania. He was born in 1810 in Ireland. He died on 03 Jan 1864 in Philadelphia, Pennsylvania.

   Peter Devlin and Susan Kennedy had the following children:

2.   i.   LUCY S.[2] DEVLIN was born on 12 Jun 1836 in Philadelphia, Pennsylvania. She died on 07 May 1909 in Gloucester City,Camden County, New Jersey. She married (1) CHRISTOPHER REITZE on 03 Mar 1855 in Philadelphia Pennsylvania. He was born on 12 Mar 1824 in Bottendorf, Kurhessen, Hesse-Cassel, Germany. He died on 16 Apr 1879 in Philadelphia, Pennsylvania. She married (2) PETER BENNER, son of Henry Benner and Mary Buser on 25 Nov 1879. He was born on 28 Oct 1824 in Philadelphia, Pennsylvania. He died on 21 Jan 1881 in Philadelphia, Pennsylvania.

3.   ii.   ISABELLA "BELLA" DEVLIN was born on 10 Feb 1839 in Philadelphia, Pennsylvania. She died on 09 Feb 1911 in Philadelphia, Philadelphia County, Pennsylvania. She married Charles F. Smith on 14 Aug 1855 in Philadelphia, Philadelphia County, Pennsylvania. He was born on 27 Jan 1831 in Germany. He died on 16 Feb 1907 in Philadelphia, Philadelphia County, Pennsylvania.

       iii.   SARAH DEVLIN was born about 1841 in Philadelphia, Pennsylvania.

       iv.   JAMES DEVLIN was born on 10 Dec 1843 in Philadelphia, Pennsylvania.

       v.   JOHN HENRY DEVLIN was born on 23 Oct 1845 in Philadelphia, Pennsylvania.

4.   vi.   MARY ANN DEVLIN was born on 04 Feb 1848 in Philadelphia, Pennsylvania. She died on 31 May 1880 in Philadelphia, Pennsylvania. She married William Wallace Thompson on 05 Sep 1870 in Philadelphia, Pennsylvania. He was born in 1842 in Philadelphia, Pennsylvania. He died after 1880.

Generation 2

2. **LUCY S.[2] DEVLIN** (Susan[1] Kennedy) was born on 12 Jun 1836 in Philadelphia, Pennsylvania. She died on 07 May 1909 in Gloucester City,Camden County, New Jersey. She married (1) **CHRISTOPHER REITZE** on 03 Mar 1855 in Philadelphia Pennsylvania. He was born on 12 Mar 1824 in Bottendorf, Kurhessen, Hesse-Cassel, Germany. He died on 16 Apr 1879 in Philadelphia, Pennsylvania. She married (2) **PETER BENNER**, son of Henry Benner and Mary Buser on 25 Nov 1879. He was born on 28 Oct 1824 in Philadelphia, Pennsylvania. He died on 21 Jan 1881 in Philadelphia, Pennsylvania.

   Christopher Reitze and Lucy S. Devlin had the following children:

5.   i.   CHRISTOPHER C.[3] REITZE JR. was born on 09 Sep 1855 in Woolwich Township, Gloucester County, New Jersey. He died on 07 Mar 1907 in Philadelphia, Pennsylvania. He married Elizabeth L. Hoffner, daughter of Thomas Hoffner and Margaret on 17 Nov 1878. She was born in Oct 1861 in Pennsylvania. She died on 31 May 1938 in Philadelphia, Pennsylvania.

       ii.   SUSAN R. REITZE was born on 12 Jan 1859. She died on 08 Aug 1859 in Philadelphia, Pennsylvania.

iii.   HENRY REITZE was born on 09 Jan 1861 in Philadelphia, Pennsylvania. He died on 28 Aug 1862 in Philadelphia, Pennsylvania.

6.   iv.   ELIZABETH M. REITZE was born on 01 Dec 1863 in Philadelphia, Pennsylvania. She died on 14 Apr 1961 in Haddonfield, Camden County, New Jersey. She married (1) EDWARD J. COLLINS, son of John Collins and Rose on 07 Nov 1882 in Philadelphia, Pennsylvania. He was born in 1859 in Pennsylvania. He died on 23 Jun 1893 in Philadelphia Pennsylvania. She married (2) HENRY GRAFE DOUGLASS, son of Henry G. Douglass and Sarah Ashton on 25 Apr 1892 in Philadelphia, Pennsylvania. He was born on 09 Jul 1854 in Philadelphia, Pennsylvania. He died on 10 Jun 1932 in Lakeland, Gloucester Township, Camden County, New Jersey.

7.   v.   CHARLES ARCHIBALD REITZE SR. was born on 07 Feb 1866 in Philadelphia, Pennsylvania. He died on 25 Sep 1893 in Philadelphia, Pennsylvania. He married Rachel M. Kelly on 04 Jan 1893 in Philadelphia, Pennsylvania. She was born about 1869 in Scotland.

8.   vi.   JOHN FRANCIS REITZE SR. was born on 30 Oct 1869 in Philadelphia, Pennsylvania. He died on 15 Feb 1955 in Philadelphia, Pennsylvania. He married (1) MARGARET CECILIA MALLOY, daughter of Martin Malloy and Catherine Kennedy on 27 Nov 1895 in Philadelphia, Pennsylvania. She was born on 25 Dec 1873 in Philadelphia, Pennsylvania. She died on 14 Oct 1918 in Philadelphia, Pennsylvania. He married (2) EMILY "EMMA" C. MALLOY, daughter of Martin Malloy and Catherine Kennedy in 1921. She was born in Oct 1888 in Pennsylvania. She died on 04 May 1951 in Philadelphia, Pennsylvania.

vii.   LUCY (TWIN) REITZE was born on 16 Mar 1872 in Philadelphia, Pennsylvania. She died on 16 Mar 1872 in Philadelphia, Pennsylvania.

viii.   WILLIAM (TWIN) REITZE was born on 16 Mar 1872 in Philadelphia, Pennsylvania. He died on 17 Mar 1872 in Philadelphia, Pennsylvania.

ix.   ELLEN (TWIN) REITZE was born on 18 Sep 1873. She died on 18 Sep 1873.

x.   JULIE (TWIN) REITZE was born on 18 Sep 1873. She died on 18 Sep 1873.

xi.   MAGGIE REITZE was born on 15 Jul 1874 in Philadelphia, Pennsylvania. She died on 20 May 1875 in Philadelphia, Pennsylvania.

xii.   CONRAD REITZE was born on 12 Mar 1876 in Philadelphia, Pennsylvania. He died on 23 Aug 1877 in Philadelphia, Pennsylvania.

9.   xiii.   JOSEPHINE IRENE REITZE was born on 04 Jul 1877 in Philadelphia, Pennsylvania. She died on 03 May 1962 in Philadelphia, Pennsylvania. She married William Scott Chambers, son of George Washington Chambers and Annie Adam Edwards on 30 Mar 1896 in Philadelphia, Pennsylvania. He was born on 05 Jun 1867 in Philadelphia, Pennsylvania. He died on 05 Feb 1950 in Philadelphia, Pennsylvania.

3.   **ISABELLA "BELLA"[2] DEVLIN** (Susan[1] Kennedy) was born on 10 Feb 1839 in Philadelphia, Pennsylvania. She died on 09 Feb 1911 in Philadelphia, Philadelphia County, Pennsylvania. She

          Appendix H

married Charles F. Smith on 14 Aug 1855 in Philadelphia, Philadelphia County, Pennsylvania. He was born on 27 Jan 1831 in Germany. He died on 16 Feb 1907 in Philadelphia, Philadelphia County, Pennsylvania.

Charles F. Smith and Isabella "Bella" Devlin had the following children:

10.   i.   GEORGE JOSEPH[3] SMITH was born on 13 Sep 1857 in Philadelphia Pennsylvania. He died on 28 Sep 1934 in Philadelphia Pennsylvania. He married (1) ROSE A. DONAHUE in 1890 in Philadelphia, Philadelphia County, Pennsylvania. She was born in Nov 1856 in Delaware. She died on 19 Mar 1901 in Philadelphia, Pennsylvania. He married (2) ANNA (--?--) about 1903. She was born about 1870 in Ireland.

          ii.   CHARLES SMITH JR. was born on 23 Jul 1858 in Philadelphia, Philadelphia County, Pennsylvania. He died on 22 Jan 1927 in Philadelphia, Philadelphia County, Pennsylvania.

          iii.   SUSAN ADELAIDE SMITH was born on 30 Sep 1860 in Philadelphia, Philadelphia. She died on 10 Aug 1864 in Philadelphia, Philadelphia County, Pennsylvania.

          iv.   FRANCIS "FRANK" SMITH was born on 12 Mar 1862 in Philadelphia, Philadelphia County, Pennsylvania. He died on 03 May 1916 in Philadelphia Pennsylvania.

11.   v.   AMELIA SMITH was born on 21 Dec 1863 in Philadelphia, Philadelphia County, Pennsylvania. She died on 26 Feb 1944 in Philadelpha, Philadelphia County, Pennsylvania. She married Thomas Aloyisius Reilly, son of John Reilly and Mary Nugent on 07 Jan 1891 in Philadelphia, Philadelphia County, Pennsylvania. He was born on 06 Jan 1859 in Philadelphia, Pennsylvania. He died on 18 Aug 1941 in Philadelphia Pennsylvania.

          vi.   MAXIMILLIAN SMITH was born about 1864 in Philadelphia, Philadelphia County, Pennsylvania. He died between 1870-1880.

          vii.   SUSAN SMITH was born about 1867 in Philadelphia, Philadelphia County, Pennsylvania. She died between 1870-1880.

12.   viii.   ELIZABETH SMITH was born on 22 Nov 1868 in Philadelphia, Philadelphia County, Pennsylvania. She died on 24 Feb 1932 in Philadelphia, Philadelphia County, Pennsylvania. She married (1) JAMES V. QUIGLEY on 02 Sep 1887 in Philadelphia, Philadelphia County, Pennsylvania. He was born on 08 Mar 1855 in Philadelphia, Pennsylvania. He died on 18 Dec 1892 in Philadelpha, Pennsylvania. She married (2) JAMES J. MCSHANE about 1905. He was born on 22 Aug 1867 in Philadelphia, Pennsylvania. He died on 06 Nov 1946 in Philadelphia, Pennsylvania.

13.   ix.   AGNES LUCY SMITH was born on 03 Mar 1869 in Philadelphia, Philadelphia County, Pennsylvania. She died on 12 Jun 1934 in Philadelphia Pennsylvania. She married Joseph Thomas Donahue on 28 Sep 1887 in Philadelphia, Philadelphia County, Pennsylvania. He was born on 21 May 1866 in Philadelphia, Pennsylvania. He died on 24 Jan 1939 in Philadelphia Pennsylvania.

          x.   WILLIAM HENRY SMITH was born in Mar 1870 in Philadelphia, Philadelphia County, Pennsylvania. He died on 05 Jun 1871 in Philadelphia, Philadelphia County, Pennsylvania.

  xi. ISABELLA SMITH was born on 09 Nov 1872 in Philadelphia, Philadelphia County, Pennsylvania. She died on 24 Apr 1873 in Philadelphia, Philadelphia County, Pennsylvania.

  xii. SARAH SMITH was born about 24 Mar 1875 in Philadelphia, Philadelphia County, Pennsylvania. She died on 26 Mar 1875 in Philadelphia, Philadelphia County, Pennsylvania.

  xiii. EMMA SMITH was born on 03 Jul 1876 in Philadelphia, Philadelphia County, Pennsylvania. She died on 09 Nov 1877 in Philadelphia, Philadelphia County, Pennsylvania.

14. xiv. JOSEPH T. SMITH was born on 22 Mar 1878 in Philadelphia, Philadelphia County, Pennsylvania. He died on 14 Jan 1945 in Philadelpha, Philadelphia County, Pennsylvania. He married (1) MARY C. DWYER, daughter of Ed Dwyer and Margaret Cox on 21 Apr 1903 in Philadelphia, Philadelphia County, Pennsylvania. She was born on 22 Apr 1881 in Philadelpha, Pennsylvania. She died on 13 Dec 1910 in Philadelphia, Pennsylvania. He married ALICE A. MALLON. She was born in 1880 in Pennsylvania. She died on 17 Apr 1935 in Philadelphia Pennsylvania.

15. xv. JOHN F. SMITH was born on 27 May 1880 in Philadelphia, Philadelphia County, Pennsylvania. He died on 11 May 1954 in Philadelphia, Philadelphia County, Pennsylvania. He married Gertrude in 1910. She was born in 1882.

  xvi. THOMAS SMITH was born on 08 May 1884 in Philadelphia, Philadelphia County, Pennsylvania. He died on 15 Jun 1884 in Philadelphia, Philadelphia County, Pennsylvania.

4. **MARY ANN[2] DEVLIN** (Susan[1] Kennedy) was born on 04 Feb 1848 in Philadelphia, Pennsylvania. She died on 31 May 1880 in Philadelphia, Pennsylvania. She married William Wallace Thompson on 05 Sep 1870 in Philadelphia, Pennsylvania. He was born in 1842 in Philadelphia, Pennsylvania. He died after 1880.

William Wallace Thompson and Mary Ann Devlin had the following children:

  i. WILLIAM "WILLIE"[3] THOMPSON was born in 1872 in Philadelphia, Pennsylvania. He died on 10 Aug 1878 in Philadelpha, Pennsylvania.

  ii. CHARLES "CHARLEY" THOMPSON was born in Mar 1874 in Philadelphia, Pennsylvania. He died on 15 Sep 1874 in Philadelphia, Pennsylvania.

  iii. SARAH "SALLIE" THOMPSON was born in Jan 1877 in Philadelphia, Pennsylvania. She died on 21 Jun 1877 in Philadelpha, Pennsylvania.

  iv. SON THOMPSON was born on 24 May 1880 in Philadelpha, Pennsylvania. He died on 24 May 1880 in Philadelpha, Pennsylvania.

Generation 3

5. **CHRISTOPHER C.[3] REITZE JR.** (Lucy S.[2] Devlin, Susan[1] Kennedy) was born on 09 Sep 1855 in Woolwich Township, Gloucester County, New Jersey. He died on 07 Mar 1907 in Philadelphia,

Pennsylvania. He married Elizabeth L. Hoffner, daughter of Thomas Hoffner and Margaret on 17 Nov 1878. She was born in Oct 1861 in Pennsylvania. She died on 31 May 1938 in Philadelphia, Pennsylvania.

Christopher C. Reitze Jr. and Elizabeth L. Hoffner had the following children:

16. i. ELIZABETH C.[4] REITZE was born on 02 Jun 1881 in Philadelphia, Pennsylvania. She died on 10 Sep 1971 in Downingtown, Uwchlan Township, Chester County, Pennsylvania 19380. She married John A. Bustard on 28 Jun 1899 in Philadelphia, Pennsylvania. He was born in Sep 1867 in Philadelphia, Pennsylvania. He died on 22 May 1934 in Philadelphia, Pennsylvania.

17. ii. MARGARET MAY REITZE was born on 02 Oct 1882 in Philadelphia, Pennsylvania. She died on 06 Jun 1959 in Gloucester Township, Camden County, New Jersey. She married Edward Taylor Burtis, son of Ellwood Burtis and Louise Diemer on 19 Jun 1901 in Philadelphia, Pennsylvania. He was born on 18 Dec 1871 in Philadelphia, Pennsylvania. He died on 23 Nov 1956 in Franklin Township, Gloucester County, New Jersey.

18. iii. CHRISTOPHER CARL REITZE I was born on 15 Sep 1885 in Philadelphia, Pennsylvania. He died on 04 Jul 1942 in Philadelphia, Pennsylvania. He married (1) HELEN C. HOENIGMANN, daughter of Peter Hoenigmann and Kathrina [Caroline Rose] on 29 Apr 1908 in Philadelphia, Pennsylvania. She was born on 20 May 1887 in Philadelphia, Pennsylvania. She died on 28 Jul 1923 in Philadelphia, Pennsylvania. He married (2) THERESA "TESS" REIMOLD, daughter of Conrad Reimold in 1924 in Philadelphia, Philadelphia County, Pennsylvania. She was born in Dec 1882 in Pennsylvania. She died on 18 Jul 1943 in Philadelphia, Pennsylvania.

6. **ELIZABETH M.**[3] **REITZE** (Lucy S.[2] Devlin, Susan[1] Kennedy) was born on 01 Dec 1863 in Philadelphia, Pennsylvania. She died on 14 Apr 1961 in Haddonfield, Camden County, New Jersey. She married (1) **EDWARD J. COLLINS**, son of John Collins and Rose on 07 Nov 1882 in Philadelphia, Pennsylvania. He was born in 1859 in Pennsylvania. He died on 23 Jun 1893 in Philadelphia Pennsylvania. She married (2) **HENRY GRAFE DOUGLASS**, son of Henry G. Douglass and Sarah Ashton on 25 Apr 1892 in Philadelphia, Pennsylvania. He was born on 09 Jul 1854 in Philadelphia, Pennsylvania. He died on 10 Jun 1932 in Lakeland, Gloucester Township, Camden County, New Jersey.

Edward J. Collins and Elizabeth M. Reitze had the following child:

 i. BABY[4] COLLINS was born on 18 Dec 1883 in Philadelphia Pennsylvania. He died on 19 Dec 1883 in Philadelphia Pennsylvania.

7. **CHARLES ARCHIBALD**[3] **REITZE SR.** (Lucy S.[2] Devlin, Susan[1] Kennedy) was born on 07 Feb 1866 in Philadelphia, Pennsylvania. He died on 25 Sep 1893 in Philadelphia, Pennsylvania. He married Rachel M. Kelly on 04 Jan 1893 in Philadelphia, Pennsylvania. She was born about 1869 in Scotland.

Charles Archibald Reitze Sr. and Rachel M. Kelly had the following child:

19. i. CHARLES ARCHIBALD[4] REITZE JR. was born on 06 Nov 1893 in Philadelphia, Pennsylvania. He died on 29 Aug 1969 in Philadelphia, Pennsylvania. He married MARY KUBICK. She was born on 04 Jul 1897 in Philadelphia, Pennsylvania. She died on 02 Jul 1964 in Philadelphia, Pennsylvania.

8.   **JOHN FRANCIS**[3] **REITZE SR.** (Lucy S.[2] Devlin, Susan[1] Kennedy) was born on 30 Oct 1869 in
     Philadelphia, Pennsylvania. He died on 15 Feb 1955 in Philadelphia, Pennsylvania. He married (1)
     MARGARET CECILIA MALLOY, daughter of Martin Malloy and Catherine Kennedy on 27 Nov 1895 in
     Philadelphia, Pennsylvania. She was born on 25 Dec 1873 in Philadelphia, Pennsylvania. She died
     on 14 Oct 1918 in Philadelphia, Pennsylvania. He married (2) **EMILY "EMMA" C. MALLOY**, daughter
     of Martin Malloy and Catherine Kennedy in 1921. She was born in Oct 1888 in Pennsylvania. She
     died on 04 May 1951 in Philadelphia, Pennsylvania.

     John Francis Reitze Sr. and Margaret Cecilia Malloy had the following children:
20.   i.   GEORGE B.[4] REITZE was born on 08 Aug 1896 in Philadelphia, Pennsylvania. He
                died about 27 Jan 1934 in Philadelphia, Pennsylvania. He married Isabel Smith in
                1924 in Philadelphia, Philadelphia County, Pennsylvania. She was born on 30 Jun
                1899. She died about 31 Dec 1978.

21.   ii.   LUCY ELIZABETH REITZE was born on 27 Nov 1897 in Pennsylvania. She died on 14
                Jun 1980 in Alameda, California 94501. She married Joshua Leon Bach, son of
                William P. Bach and Mary B. Yurgey in 1917 in Philadelphia, Philadelphia County,
                Pennsylvania. He was born on 21 Apr 1890 in Pottstown, Pennsylvania. He died on
                21 May 1951 in Alameda, California 94501.

         iii.   JOHN FRANCIS REITZE JR. was born on 23 Nov 1901 in Pennsylvania. He died on 20
                Feb 1975 in Philadelphia, Pennsylvania.

22.   iv.   CATHERINE IRENE REITZE was born on 04 Sep 1903 in Philadelphia, Pennsylvania.
                She died on 21 Mar 1995 in West Caldwell, Essex County, New Jersey. She
                married Frank John Kelly in 1925 in Philadelphia, Philadelphia County,
                Pennsylvania. He was born in 1901 in Pennsylvania.

23.   v.   ELIZABETH MARY REITZE was born on 01 Sep 1905 in Philadelphia, Pennsylvania.
                She died on 27 Apr 1957 in Philadelphia, Pennsylvania. She married John Joseph
                Page Sr. in Sep 1925 in Philadelphia, Pennsylvania. He was born on 12 Oct 1902 in
                Philadelphia, Pennsylvania. He died on 17 Jan 1971 in Philadelphia, Pennsylvania.

9.   **JOSEPHINE IRENE**[3] **REITZE** (Lucy S.[2] Devlin, Susan[1] Kennedy) was born on 04 Jul 1877 in
     Philadelphia, Pennsylvania. She died on 03 May 1962 in Philadelphia, Pennsylvania. She married
     William Scott Chambers, son of George Washington Chambers and Annie Adam Edwards on 30
     Mar 1896 in Philadelphia, Pennsylvania. He was born on 05 Jun 1867 in Philadelphia,
     Pennsylvania. He died on 05 Feb 1950 in Philadelphia, Pennsylvania.

     William Scott Chambers and Josephine Irene Reitze had the following children:
24.   i.   HENRY GRAFE[4] CHAMBERS was born on 08 Jan 1897 in Philadelphia, Pennsylvania.
                He died on 11 Nov 1953 in Collingswood, Camden County, New Jersey. He married
                Mary Ann McCauley, daughter of Thomas McCauley and Mary Ann Wallace on 30
                Jul 1918 in Philadelphia, Pennsylvania. She was born on 07 Jul 1892 in
                Philadelphia, Pennsylvania. She died on 08 Aug 1984 in Burlington Township,
                Burlington County, New Jersey.

25.   ii.   LUCY ELIZABETH CHAMBERS was born on 11 Mar 1898 in Philadelphia, Pennsylvania.
                She died on 22 Nov 1918 in Philadelphia, Pennsylvania. She married William
                Thompson, son of William Thompson and Hester Carrick on 12 Jun 1915 in Elkton,
                Cecil County, Maryland. He was born on 28 May 1891 in Pennsylvania. He died on

19 Jun 1965 in Philadelphia, Pennsylvania.

10. GEORGE JOSEPH[3] SMITH (Isabella "Bella"[2] Devlin, Susan[1] Kennedy) was born on 13 Sep 1857 in Philadelphia Pennsylvania. He died on 28 Sep 1934 in Philadelphia Pennsylvania. He married (1) ROSE A. DONAHUE in 1890 in Philadelphia, Philadelphia County, Pennsylvania. She was born in Nov 1856 in Delaware. She died on 19 Mar 1901 in Philadelphia, Pennsylvania. He married (2) ANNA (--?--) about 1903. She was born about 1870 in Ireland.

George Joseph Smith and Rose A. Donahue had the following child:
26. i. HUGH CHARLES[4] SMITH was born on 23 Jul 1893 in Philadelphia, Pennsylvania. He died on 01 Apr 1938 in Philadelpha, Pennsylvania. He married MARY I GALLAGHER. She was born on 29 Jul 1894 in Philadelphia, Pennsylvania. She died on 10 Jan 1943 in Philadelphia, Pennsylvania.

11. AMELIA[3] SMITH (Isabella "Bella"[2] Devlin, Susan[1] Kennedy) was born on 21 Dec 1863 in Philadelphia, Philadelphia County, Pennsylvania. She died on 26 Feb 1944 in Philadelpha, Philadelphia County, Pennsylvania. She married Thomas Aloyisius Reilly, son of John Reilly and Mary Nugent on 07 Jan 1891 in Philadelphia, Philadelphia County, Pennsylvania. He was born on 06 Jan 1859 in Philadelphia, Pennsylvania. He died on 18 Aug 1941 in Philadelphia Pennsylvania.

Thomas Aloyisius Reilly and Amelia Smith had the following children:
i. JOHN J.[4] REILLY was born on 06 Nov 1891 in Philadelphia, Pennsylvania. He died after 1917.

27. ii. HELEN REILLY was born on 14 Jan 1894 in Philadelphia, Pennsylvania. She died on 07 Apr 1958 in Philadelphia, Pennsylvania. She married John Blankley in 1920.

iii. ISABELLA REILLY was born on 23 Nov 1895. She died on 23 Jan 1899 in Philadelphia, Pennsylvania.

12. ELIZABETH[3] SMITH (Isabella "Bella"[2] Devlin, Susan[1] Kennedy) was born on 22 Nov 1868 in Philadelphia, Philadelphia County, Pennsylvania. She died on 24 Feb 1932 in Philadelphia, Philadelphia County, Pennsylvania. She married (1) JAMES V. QUIGLEY on 02 Sep 1887 in Philadelphia, Philadelphia County, Pennsylvania. He was born on 08 Mar 1855 in Philadelphia, Pennsylvania. He died on 18 Dec 1892 in Philadelpha, Pennsylvania. She married (2) JAMES J. MCSHANE about 1905. He was born on 22 Aug 1867 in Philadelphia, Pennsylvania. He died on 06 Nov 1946 in Philadelphia, Pennsylvania.

James V. Quigley and Elizabeth Smith had the following child:
i. CATHARINE[4] QUIGLEY was born in 1889 in Pennsylvania. She died after 1910.

13. AGNES LUCY[3] SMITH (Isabella "Bella"[2] Devlin, Susan[1] Kennedy) was born on 03 Mar 1869 in Philadelphia, Philadelphia County, Pennsylvania. She died on 12 Jun 1934 in Philadelphia Pennsylvania. She married Joseph Thomas Donahue on 28 Sep 1887 in Philadelphia, Philadelphia County, Pennsylvania. He was born on 21 May 1866 in Philadelphia, Pennsylvania. He died on 24 Jan 1939 in Philadelphia Pennsylvania.

Joseph Thomas Donahue and Agnes Lucy Smith had the following children:
i. CHARLES[4] DONAHUE was born on 29 Dec 1887 in Philadelphia, Philadelphia County, Pennsylvania.

      ii.   AGNES DONAHUE was born on 05 Mar 1889 in Philadelphia, Philadelphia County, Pennsylvania.

      iii.   JOSEPH DONAHUE was born on 07 Oct 1890 in Philadelphia, Philadelphia County, Pennsylvania. He died on 14 Oct 1890 in Philadelphia, Philadelphia County, Pennsylvania.

28.   iv.   SARAH DONAHUE was born on 01 Jan 1892 in Philadelphia, Philadelphia County, Pennsylvania. She died in 1967. She married JAMES THOMAS CRAWFORD. He was born in 1891. He died in 1966.

      v.   THOMAS DONAHUE was born on 27 Dec 1896 in Philadelphia, Philadelphia County, Pennsylvania.

      vi.   FRANCIS DONAHUE was born on 02 Apr 1897 in Philadelphia, Philadelphia County, Pennsylvania.

      vii.   ISABEL DONAHUE was born in 1904.

      viii.   JOHN DONAHUE was born in 1907.

      ix.   JOSEPH DONAHUE was born in 1910.

14.   **JOSEPH T.**[3] **SMITH** (Isabella "Bella"[2] Devlin, Susan[1] Kennedy) was born on 22 Mar 1878 in Philadelphia, Philadelphia County, Pennsylvania. He died on 14 Jan 1945 in Philadelpha, Philadelphia County, Pennsylvania. He married (1) **MARY C. DWYER**, daughter of Ed Dwyer and Margaret Cox on 21 Apr 1903 in Philadelphia, Philadelphia County, Pennsylvania. She was born on 22 Apr 1881 in Philadelpha, Pennsylvania. She died on 13 Dec 1910 in Philadelphia, Pennsylvania. He married **ALICE A. MALLON**. She was born in 1880 in Pennsylvania. She died on 17 Apr 1935 in Philadelphia Pennsylvania.

Joseph T. Smith and Mary C. Dwyer had the following children:

      i.   CHARLES[4] SMITH was born on 12 Feb 1904 in Philadelphia Pennsylvania.

      ii.   JOSEPH SMITH was born on 12 Jul 1905 in Philadelphia Pennsylvania. He died on 07 Jan 1907 in Philadelphia Pennsylvania.

      iii.   EDWARD SMITH was born on 25 Aug 1906 in Philadelphia Pennsylvania.

29.   iv.   FRANCIS ALOYSIUS SMITH was born on 01 Oct 1908 in Philadelphia Pennsylvania. He died in May 1976 in Philadelphia, Pennsylvania. He married PARCETTA DIMATTEO. She was born in 1906 in New York. She died in 1989 in Philadelphia, Pennsylvania.

      v.   MARGARET SMITH was born in 1910 in Philadelphia Pennsylvania.

Joseph T. Smith and Alice A. Mallon had the following children:

      vi.   ALICE SMITH was born in 1917 in Philadelphia Pennsylvania.

    vii.   JOSEPH SMITH was born in 1919 in Philadelphia Pennsylvania.

15.   JOHN F.[3] SMITH (Isabella "Bella"[2] Devlin, Susan[1] Kennedy) was born on 27 May 1880 in Philadelphia, Philadelphia County, Pennsylvania. He died on 11 May 1954 in Philadelphia, Philadelphia County, Pennsylvania. He married Gertrude in 1910. She was born in 1882.

John F. Smith and Gertrude had the following children:

    i.   FRANCIS[4] SMITH was born in 1912 in Philadelphia, Pennsylvania.

    ii.   GERTRUDE SMITH was born in 1914 in Philadelphia, Pennsylvania.

    iii.   BEATRICE SMITH was born in 1916 in Philadelphia, Pennsylvania.

    iv.   JOHN SMITH was born in 1918 in Philadelphia, Pennsylvania.

    v.   DOROTHY SMITH was born in 1919 in Philadelphia, Pennsylvania.

Generation 4

16.   ELIZABETH C.[4] REITZE (Christopher C.[3] Jr., Lucy S.[2] Devlin, Susan[1] Kennedy) was born on 02 Jun 1881 in Philadelphia, Pennsylvania. She died on 10 Sep 1971 in Downingtown, Uwchlan Township, Chester County, Pennsylvania 19380. She married John A. Bustard on 28 Jun 1899 in Philadelphia, Pennsylvania. He was born in Sep 1867 in Philadelphia, Pennsylvania. He died on 22 May 1934 in Philadelphia, Pennsylvania.

John A. Bustard and Elizabeth C. Reitze had the following children:

    i.   EDWARD JOHN[5] BUSTARD was born on 15 Jan 1901 in Philadelphia, Pennsylvania. He died on 16 Apr 1927 in Philadelphia, Pennsylvania. He married Helen Weber about Aug 1926 in Philadelphia, Pennsylvania.

    ii.   CHRISTOPHER C. BUSTARD was born on 03 Jul 1904 in Philadelphia, Pennsylvania. He died on 10 Sep 1942 in North Atlantic Ocean (World War II). He married Dora Rhettenbock in 1927 in Philadelphia, Philadelphia County, Pennsylvania. She was born on 25 Mar 1906. She died on 02 Sep 1972.

    iii.   ELIZABETH WRAY BUSTARD was born on 02 May 1906 in Philadelphia, Pennsylvania. She died on 30 May 1981 in Downingtown, Uwchlan Township, Chester County, Pennsylvania. She married ROBERT WILSON. He was born in 1901 in Montana. He died on 02 Aug 1959 in Butte, Silver Bow, Montana.

17.   MARGARET MAY[4] REITZE (Christopher C.[3] Jr., Lucy S.[2] Devlin, Susan[1] Kennedy) was born on 02 Oct 1882 in Philadelphia, Pennsylvania. She died on 06 Jun 1959 in Gloucester Township, Camden County, New Jersey. She married Edward Taylor Burtis, son of Ellwood Burtis and Louise Diemer on 19 Jun 1901 in Philadelphia, Pennsylvania. He was born on 18 Dec 1871 in Philadelphia, Pennsylvania. He died on 23 Nov 1956 in Franklin Township, Gloucester County, New Jersey.

Edward Taylor Burtis and Margaret May Reitze had the following children:

    i.   ELLWOOD C.[5] BURTIS was born in Apr 1903 in Philadelphia, Pennsylvania. He died on 27 Mar 1904 in Philadelphia, Pennsylvania.

ii. MILDRED BURTIS was born in 1907 in Philadelphia, Pennsylvania. She married LEON MCCOY SR..

iii. ELSIE BURTIS was born on 03 May 1910. She died on 24 Sep 1999 in Leesburg, Florida. She married (1) ARNOLD J. BRYAN in 1927 in Philadelphia, Philadelphia County, Pennsylvania. He was born in 1910. He died on 15 Feb 1972. She married (2) HAIG SAHAG MEDZARENTZ about 1977. He was born on 23 Feb 1923 in Philadelphia, Pennsylvania. He died on 03 Jun 2015 in Bushnell, Florida.

iv. ELIZABETH BURTIS was born on 04 Aug 1914. She died on 05 May 1961. She married Howard Prince Sr. on 23 Mar 1934. He was born on 30 Jul 1912. He died on 18 Nov 1961.

18. **CHRISTOPHER CARL[4] REITZE I** (Christopher C.[3] Jr., Lucy S.[2] Devlin, Susan[1] Kennedy) was born on 15 Sep 1885 in Philadelphia, Pennsylvania. He died on 04 Jul 1942 in Philadelphia, Pennsylvania. He married (1) **HELEN C. HOENIGMANN**, daughter of Peter Hoenigmann and Kathrina [Caroline Rose] on 29 Apr 1908 in Philadelphia, Pennsylvania. She was born on 20 May 1887 in Philadelphia, Pennsylvania. She died on 28 Jul 1923 in Philadelphia, Pennsylvania. He married (2) **THERESA "TESS" REIMOLD**, daughter of Conrad Reimold in 1924 in Philadelphia, Philadelphia County, Pennsylvania. She was born in Dec 1882 in Pennsylvania. She died on 18 Jul 1943 in Philadelphia, Pennsylvania.

Christopher Carl Reitze I and Helen C. Hoenigmann had the following children:

i. CHRISTOPHER CARL[5] REITZE II was born on 19 Nov 1909 in Philadelphia, Pennsylvania. He died on 05 Feb 1985 in Pittsburgh, Allegheny County, Pennsylvania. He married (1) MARGARET MCFADDEN on 15 May 1930 in Philadelphia, Pennsylvania. She was born on 02 Jan 1906. She died on 20 May 1973 in Pittsburgh, Allegheny County, Pennsylvania. He married (2) HELEN SHOEMAKER after 1973.

ii. HARRY EDWIN REITZE SR. was born on 19 Jun 1919 in Philadelphia, Pennsylvania. He died on 16 Sep 1999 in Concord, New Hampshire. He married Jeanne Helene Chamberland on 12 Sep 1959 in Philadelphia, Pennsylvania. She was born on 07 Jan 1927 in Manchester, New Hampshire. She died on 25 Jun 2009.

19. **CHARLES ARCHIBALD[4] REITZE JR.** (Charles Archibald[3] Sr., Lucy S.[2] Devlin, Susan[1] Kennedy) was born on 06 Nov 1893 in Philadelphia, Pennsylvania. He died on 29 Aug 1969 in Philadelphia, Pennsylvania. He married **MARY KUBICK**. She was born on 04 Jul 1897 in Philadelphia, Pennsylvania. She died on 02 Jul 1964 in Philadelphia, Pennsylvania.

Charles Archibald Reitze Jr. and Mary Kubick had the following child:

i. JOHN C.[5] REITZ was born on 18 Nov 1928 in Philadelphia, Pennsylvania. He died on 01 Dec 1972 in Lansdale, Montgomery, Pennsylvania, USA. He married ELEANOR MARY WITOSLAWSKI. She was born on 09 Jul 1925. She died on 08 Jan 1995.

20. **GEORGE B.[4] REITZE** (John Francis[3] Sr., Lucy S.[2] Devlin, Susan[1] Kennedy) was born on 08 Aug 1896 in Philadelphia, Pennsylvania. He died about 27 Jan 1934 in Philadelphia, Pennsylvania. He married Isabel Smith in 1924 in Philadelphia, Philadelphia County, Pennsylvania. She was born on 30 Jun 1899. She died about 31 Dec 1978.

George B. Reitze and Isabel Smith had the following child:

    i.   GEORGE J.[5] REITZE was born on 26 Dec 1926 in Philadelphia, Pennsylvania. He died about 19 Sep 1983 in Delaware County, PA 19063. He married ANNE HAEFFNER.

21.   LUCY ELIZABETH[4] REITZE (John Francis[3] Sr., Lucy S.[2] Devlin, Susan[1] Kennedy) was born on 27 Nov 1897 in Pennsylvania. She died on 14 Jun 1980 in Alameda, California 94501. She married Joshua Leon Bach, son of William P. Bach and Mary B. Yurgey in 1917 in Philadelphia, Philadelphia County, Pennsylvania. He was born on 21 Apr 1890 in Pottstown, Pennsylvania. He died on 21 May 1951 in Alameda, California 94501.

Joshua Leon Bach and Lucy Elizabeth Reitze had the following children:
    i.   JAY LEON[5] BACH was born on 14 Dec 1922 in Baltimore, Maryland. He died on 28 May 1943 in Plumas County, California (World War II).

    ii.   LOUIS BACH was born on 31 Oct 1927 in Baltimore, Maryland. He died on 21 Sep 1985 in Sonoma County, California.

22.   CATHERINE IRENE[4] REITZE (John Francis[3] Sr., Lucy S.[2] Devlin, Susan[1] Kennedy) was born on 04 Sep 1903 in Philadelphia, Pennsylvania. She died on 21 Mar 1995 in West Caldwell, Essex County, New Jersey. She married Frank John Kelly in 1925 in Philadelphia, Philadelphia County, Pennsylvania. He was born in 1901 in Pennsylvania.

Frank John Kelly and Catherine Irene Reitze had the following children:
    i.   FRANK[5] KELLY JR. was born on 29 Apr 1926 in Philadelphia, Pennsylvania. He died on 31 Oct 1993 in Jupiter, Palm Beach County, FL 33477. He married GRACE. He married SECOND WIFE.

    ii.   MARGARET KELLY was born on 17 Jun 1927 in Philadelphia, Pennsylvania. She married HERBERT BURNS.

23.   ELIZABETH MARY[4] REITZE (John Francis[3] Sr., Lucy S.[2] Devlin, Susan[1] Kennedy) was born on 01 Sep 1905 in Philadelphia, Pennsylvania. She died on 27 Apr 1957 in Philadelphia, Pennsylvania. She married John Joseph Page Sr. in Sep 1925 in Philadelphia, Pennsylvania. He was born on 12 Oct 1902 in Philadelphia, Pennsylvania. He died on 17 Jan 1971 in Philadelphia, Pennsylvania.

John Joseph Page Sr. and Elizabeth Mary Reitze had the following children:
    i.   JOHN JOSEPH[5] PAGE JR. was born on 15 Sep 1926 in Philadelphia, Pennsylvania.

    ii.   JAMES GEORGE PAGE was born on 16 Aug 1933 in Philadelphia, Pennsylvania. He died on 13 Jan 2003 in Doraville, Georgia. He married Barbara Summerill on 06 Oct 1962 in Philadelphia, Pennsylvania. She was born on 01 Feb 1941 in Philadelphia, Pennsylvania.

24.   HENRY GRAFE[4] CHAMBERS (Josephine Irene[3] Reitze, Lucy S.[2] Devlin, Susan[1] Kennedy) was born on 08 Jan 1897 in Philadelphia, Pennsylvania. He died on 11 Nov 1953 in Collingswood, Camden County, New Jersey. He married Mary Ann McCauley, daughter of Thomas McCauley and Mary Ann Wallace on 30 Jul 1918 in Philadelphia, Pennsylvania. She was born on 07 Jul 1892 in Philadelphia, Pennsylvania. She died on 08 Aug 1984 in Burlington Township, Burlington County, New Jersey.

Henry Grafe Chambers and Mary Ann McCauley had the following children:

    i.   WILLIAM SCOTT[5] CHAMBERS was born on 25 Feb 1921 in Philadelphia, Pennsylvania. He died on 08 Feb 2014 in Plantation Broward County Florida. He married Gloria Ann Freda, daughter of Guerino Angelo Maria Freda and Filomena M. Quaresima on 26 Jan 1946 in Princeton, Mercer County, New Jersey. She was born on 06 Mar 1921 in Princeton, Mercer County, New Jersey. She died on 28 Aug 1987 in Portsmouth, Virginia.

    ii.   THOMAS WALLACE CHAMBERS was born on 25 Mar 1923 in Philadelphia, Pennsylvania. He died on 06 Oct 1955 in Stateburg, Sumter County, South Carolina. He married Florence Clark, daughter of James Freeman Clark and Anna Lee on 31 May 1948 in New Castle, New Castle County, Delaware. She was born on 13 Apr 1930 in Haddonfield, Camden County, New Jersey. She died on 16 Feb 2016 in Churchville, Bucks County, Pennsylvania.

25.   LUCY ELIZABETH[4] CHAMBERS (Josephine Irene[3] Reitze, Lucy S.[2] Devlin, Susan[1] Kennedy) was born on 11 Mar 1898 in Philadelphia, Pennsylvania. She died on 22 Nov 1918 in Philadelphia, Pennsylvania. She married William Thompson, son of William Thompson and Hester Carrick on 12 Jun 1915 in Elkton, Cecil County, Maryland. He was born on 28 May 1891 in Pennsylvania. He died on 19 Jun 1965 in Philadelphia, Pennsylvania.

William Thompson and Lucy Elizabeth Chambers had the following child:

    i.   JOSEPHINE HESTER[5] THOMPSON was born on 10 May 1916 in Philadelphia, Pennsylvania. She died on 06 Oct 2008 in Haddonfield, Camden County, New Jersey. She married David Harrington Marshall Sr., son of Thomas Marshall on 13 Jun 1942 in Philadelphia, Pennsylvania. He was born on 27 Jun 1912 in Philadelphia, Pennsylvania. He died on 02 Nov 2009 in Newark, Delaware.

26.   HUGH CHARLES[4] SMITH (George Joseph[3], Isabella "Bella"[2] Devlin, Susan[1] Kennedy) was born on 23 Jul 1893 in Philadelphia, Pennsylvania. He died on 01 Apr 1938 in Philadelpha, Pennsylvania. He married **MARY I GALLAGHER**. She was born on 29 Jul 1894 in Philadelphia, Pennsylvania. She died on 10 Jan 1943 in Philadelphia, Pennsylvania.

Hugh Charles Smith and Mary I Gallagher had the following children:

    i.   HELEN[5] SMITH was born in 1916.

    ii.   GEORGE SMITH was born in 1918.

    iii.   MARIE SMITH was born in 1921.

    iv.   MARGARET SMITH was born in 1924.

27.   HELEN[4] REILLY (Amelia[3] Smith, Isabella "Bella"[2] Devlin, Susan[1] Kennedy) was born on 14 Jan 1894 in Philadelphia, Pennsylvania. She died on 07 Apr 1958 in Philadelphia, Pennsylvania. She married John Blankley in 1920.

John Blankley and Helen Reilly had the following children:

    i.   HELEN[5] BLANKLEY was born in 1924 in Philadelpha, Pennsylvania.

    ii.   MARION BLANKLEY was born in 1928 in Philadelpha, Pennsylvania.

28. **SARAH**[4] **DONAHUE** (Agnes Lucy[3] Smith, Isabella "Bella"[2] Devlin, Susan[1] Kennedy) was born on 01 Jan 1892 in Philadelphia, Philadelphia County, Pennsylvania. She died in 1967. She married **JAMES THOMAS CRAWFORD**. He was born in 1891. He died in 1966.

James Thomas Crawford and Sarah Donahue had the following child:
   i.   REGINA[5] CRAWFORD.

29. **FRANCIS ALOYSIUS**[4] **SMITH** (Joseph T.[3], Isabella "Bella"[2] Devlin, Susan[1] Kennedy) was born on 01 Oct 1908 in Philadelphia Pennsylvania. He died in May 1976 in Philadelphia, Pennsylvania. He married **PARCETTA DIMATTEO**. She was born in 1906 in New York. She died in 1989 in Philadelphia, Pennsylvania.

Francis Aloysius Smith and Parcetta DiMatteo had the following children:
   i.   REGINA[5] SMITH was born in 1938 in New York. She married PETER BRIGLIA.

   ii. VERONICA SMITH was born in 1941. She died on 17 Apr 2005 in Mays Landing, New Jersey. She married THOMAS J. FALZANI.

INDEX

INDEX

www.ingramcontent.com/pod-product-compliance
Lightning Source LLC
Chambersburg PA
CBHW081619250726
48657CB00009B/2633